Zing!™

21 Insights on Maximizing Your Influence

21 Insights on Maximizing Your Influence

Nancy Hunter Denney

Leadership
Development Systems, LLC

Just add people.

Marion, Massachusetts

Published by Zing! Leadership Development Systems, LLC.
Cover Design by Josh Visser
Text Layout by Corryn Hurst

To Order Books or Inquire about Group Sales:
www.zingleadership.com

Distributed by:
Zing! Leadership Development Systems, LLC
Box 1041
Marion, MA 02738
888.566.7536

Library of Congress Cataloging-in-Publication Data
Denney, Nancy Hunter, 1960-
    Zing! 21 Insights on Maximizing Your Influence/ Nancy Hunter Denney
    ISBN-13: 978-0-9792134-2-7
    ISBN-10: 0-9792134-2-8
1. Leadership. 2. Motivation. 3. Business.

Printed in the United States of America

This book is dedicated to those who have the insights to seek happiness, play in the rain, love their family and friends, show grace in the face of adversity, follow their heart, believe in the power of prayer, value what they have while they have it; and make the world a better place through their presence.

For my life and leadership, I dedicate this book to my loving husband, Tom, precious children, Kaitlin and Jake, dear parents, Rosalie and Chip Hunter, and to my favorite mother-in-law, Edith Denney. With special dedication to my incredible sisters, Barbara Quinn, Elizabeth Price, and Gabrielle Miller – women of many insights.

TABLE OF CONTENTS

FOREWORD

You are going to find great enjoyment, direction, and Zing!, in reading this book. It provides an immediate positive charge to your attitude and outlook on life, because it is packed with the punch of collective voices spoken by one dedicated educator, and difference maker. If you want to take your life and leadership to higher levels, this book will teach you not only why, but how to override competing forces to positively influence others.

Zing! is a practical and insightful guide for individuals dedicated to making the world a better place, one person, company, neighborhood, or organization, at a time. In a unique approach, Nancy Hunter Denney has studied various leadership models, ideas, principles, laws, practices, and even a few "fish tales," from leadership and motivational experts around the country to arrive at twenty-one INSIGHTS necessary for *Zing!* – a term she uses to symbolize positive influence, energy, and personal magnetism or charisma.

Whether for personal, family, community, or professional use, the anecdotes and examples provided in this book will hit a personal cord. Nancy speaks directly to you – the reader – as if you were seated next to her. Her optimism in the future is apparent, as is her challenge to your leadership and life potential.

Throughout every page, Nancy asks tough questions, tells great stories, and guides you down a path of higher character, happiness, and clarity of purpose. With this understanding you can plant positive seeds of hope, love, encouragement, and faith.

As a result of reading *Zing!* you will be encouraged to not only live your life for a greater good, but will possess the most significant tools needed to start, re-direct, or continue, your work. Nancy has given you literally hundreds of tips, skill-building lessons, and opportunities for self-introspection, designed to jump start more productive attitudes and behaviors.

God has given us all special gifts, but they are not for us alone. Our gifts are meant to bless the lives of others, and that's what making a difference is about. My friend, Nancy Hunter Denney, has done a super-fantastic job of discussing leadership as the process of making a difference. Enjoy.

- Keith Harrell, Author of *Attitude is Everything*

ACKNOWLEDGEMENTS

I don't think it's possible to achieve many things in life on your own; whether writing a book, graduating from high school or succeeding in life. Over the past few years, the development of *Zing! 21 Insights on Maximizing Your Influence* has been advanced by the thousands of college students, health care professionals, parents, educators, emerging leaders and association professionals who have enthusiastically embraced the energy of Zing! and brought it to their homes, communities, organizations, schools and lives. They have offered feedback, examples and appreciation for the inspiration accompanying Zing! claiming it has raised the bar on their life and leadership. I am most appreciative and honored they have kept the contagious positive energy of Zing! alive.

My children are now teenagers and on the edge of going off to college – a place I know well. I thank them for providing their insights on the challenges and blessings of trying to grow up in a world they didn't create; I am grateful for their sense of ownership for the future. Despite wanting to take credit for their sense of civic engagement, I acknowledge the many caring neighbors, church members, adult friends, sailing coaches, parents of their friends, teachers and grandparents who have positively influenced my children's lives over these extremely impressionable teenage years. I am especially grateful to the high caliber of committed educators and school administrators at Bishop Stang High School, Dartmouth, MA, whose daily interaction with our future leaders and citizens is making the world a better place. They continue to demonstrate Zing! by proving you can teach teenagers how to build character, grow in faith, serve all of mankind, respect others, learn in community, and achieve academic excellence.

I also want to recognize those people who I continue to watch closely. The Zing! people in my life who never cease to amaze me as they seek nothing for themselves and graciously serve others. By observing them, I have learned important lessons – many of which are shared in the pages to follow: Ms. Diane Willis, Ms. Kari Eisenhooth, Dr. Will Keim, Mr. Marlon Smith, Dr. Dennis Black, Dr. Maureen Hartford, Mr. Johnny Tuitel, Dr. Susan Salvador, Mrs. Janet Richardson, Dr. Judy Robinson, Ms. Teri Bump, Rev. Bob MacFarlane, Mo Bowen, David Fortin, Herb and Jori Borden, and Jack from The General Store. Life long admiration goes out to: Dr. Ralph Iannuzzi, Dr. Robert Maloney, Dr. Jason Reynolds, and the Reverand Jim Rand.

Special appreciation is extended to: Josh Visser of Visser Graphics for his continued professionalism and creative genius; the wonderful individuals at Color House Graphics; Corryn Hurst for her excellence in layout and design work; and to George Ranville of Alternatives in Motion for his continued support.

Finally, enormous amounts of thanks are extended to my editor in chief, Thomas Denney, whose unconditional support throughout the editing of this second edition (and my career) has been the greatest influence of all.

INTRODUCTION

This is the second edition of Zing! written four years after the first edition was published. It is considerably different than the original writing of 2004 because much has happened in the past few years. The world has changed around me and in response, I've changed. What I thought was an effective strategy of influence worked then, but not now. What seemed like a reasonable response to overcoming obstacles, isn't enough now. When things change, it's time to change!

Zing! is an approach to life that asks you to respond to what's going on in your environment, including those in it. The goal of Zing! is to bring you enhanced happiness by raising your personal expectations for life and leadership. Operating on the premise, "the energy you put out there is the energy you get to draw from," Zing! inspires a positive outlook on life and offers an equation to better understand how all the pieces of personal effectiveness and performance come together. With Zing! also comes the internal motivation to be a better observer of life and more aware of how you are being perceived by those you intentionally (and unintentionally) influence or lead. Serving a greater social good continues to be the ultimate desired outcome of Zing!.

Some of the original thoughts offered in the first edition have been updated or revised in response to new obstacles and challenges, as well as, the ever changing demographics of my speaking audiences who continue to provide all the material I could ever need. The 21 Insights have remained the same because they continue to be effective strategies for becoming more personally magnetic to others and more influential. One of the more significant changes to this edition of Zing! centers around the use of alternative leadership perspectives – specifically, charismatic leadership. As this area of study shifts from the more flamboyant self-serving image of charismatic individuals, to inspiring research validating the traits of successful charismatic leaders, it provides enhanced insight and supportive evidence into why people follow certain people.

The best thing about writing a second edition of this – or any book – is it proves one of the Zing! beliefs: You do get a second chance to make a good first impression.

Chapter 1

IT'S ZING! TIME

"You can't move people to action unless you first move them with emotion. The heart comes before the head."
- John C. Maxwell

When you wake up one day with the revelation: You wouldn't hang out with you if you didn't have to – it's time. If the blandness in your world is brightened up by adding more beige – it's time. No more complaining you are consistently overlooked, underpaid or bored. No more compartmentalizing the various aspects of your life (i.e. your marriage, friendships, parenting, career, involvements or academic pursuits) because it prevents you from having to be honest about the *overall* quality of your life. Despite the many things you've accomplished in your lifetime, if you are tired of feeling invisible, average, or perceived by others as "less than," the time has come to take control of your destiny and maximize your potential for greater happiness. To summarize: It's Zing! time.

Definition of Zing!

Zing! is an "approach, attitude and action package" for making yourself more influential and productive with the ultimate goal of making the world a better place. It is not only a mindset, but the translation of that mindset into actions, positive energy and influence. Zing! is a way to live and lead through enhanced confidence and charisma which necessitates living and leading with an exclamation point. By definition, *Zing!* is "the ability to override competing forces to positively influence others towards a greater social good." Zing! is the "it" you wish you had when you needed it!

The Zing! People

There are people who just seem to naturally come by Zing! or "it." Described as "the movers and shakers," "up and coming superstars" or "going places people," these individuals have a unique ability to make things happen. They possess a clear and unique sense of self – free from insecurity, doubt and excuses, and appear self-confident, determined, and spiritual while maintaining an authentic sense of self. Life itself is a gift they cherish and intentionally put to good use. Leadership is viewed as a blessing, not a burden.

Like the invisible force of a magnet, people working on their Zing! (such as students, parents, educators, professors, business leaders, employees, or anyone wanting more out of life) effortlessly draw you into their world; get you to support their ideas or motivate you to embrace their vision. Their techniques are intriguing, if you can actually describe what they possess as a "technique" in the first place. There seems to be more to their personal magnetism than the positions of leadership or influential status they seek or hold. Is it a personality thing or natural charisma? Is it their relationship building skills? Is it the predictability of their actions? When around such individuals, you can't help but feel a sense of "reverence" towards them or be in "awe."

Those who have "it" – this thing called Zing! – leave those around them feeling better about themselves, more energized and inspired. You want to be around them – even like them. In their presence you feel welcomed, valued and worthy. You feel as if your opinions count and your life matters to them. This conclusion is reached because they are genuinely more interested in your goals and direction in life than talking about their own. Despite the fact these appealing personalities have many different kinds of relationships, and are often very well connected, their appeal is enhanced by the fact they always take time to connect with complete strangers, as well as, with those they know.

One of the most significant characteristics of someone with Zing! is their ability to never make someone feel like a distraction, interruption or "less than" anyone else in their world. They clearly treat you with unconditional positive regard, and provide equal access to the people they know. Amazingly, they can walk into a room of one hundred people and make each feel as if they are the most important person in the room!

Those with this unique ability to *override competing forces to positively influence others* clearly want to share the wealth. It's not about them; it's about doing good things for others and proceeding with a collective spirit, not one rooted in competition. Accompany Zing! is a clear sense of purpose; to enthusiastically (and often quietly) empower others by enhancing their feelings of self-efficacy and ownership in any number of outcomes. When around people with Zing! you might have a natural tendency to be skeptical or proceed with caution, yet it's surprisingly effortless to whole heartedly trust their intentions without really knowing why.

Zing! is not an evil "power" or some kind of "spell" found in people like Ken Lay of Enron, Bernie Ebbers of WorldCom, or Frank Lorenzo of Eastern Air Lines who used their apparent charisma to build blind faith in their abilities, then proceed to ruin so many lives and leave hard working employees without retirement benefits. Zing! comes with a moral responsibility; an awareness and respect for their potential influence and accept the opportunity, as well as, the obligation, to make a positive difference in the world.

At the very heart of people with Zing! is concern for the welfare of society, raising up those less fortunate and using their talents, resources and time to leave the world better than they found it. Whether they flip burgers at McDonalds or spread sheets on Wall Street, there is room in their lives to make others better people, spread encouragement and be productive contributing members of society. They are the leaders and the followers who know the truth: "The one with the most toys at the end of the day doesn't know how to share!" It is from a place of abundance, not scarcity they live, and consequently, lead.

From a personal perspective, Zing! individuals often gain reverence and respect because they have overcome the tragedies, hardships, and challenges life has given them with a huge amount of grace; choosing not to ask, "Why me?" or complain. They rarely notice what materialistic possessions they lack and others appear to have. Their life story is used to help others get through *their* struggles with less pain; an approach clearly rooted in a powerful faith, a belief in treating people equally, and in a strong commitment to keeping their lives simple. Family is a priority. Not only do they donate their time and talents, they give of their resources.

Discovering the Benefits of Zing!

Zing! can be the driving force – or energy – behind your life and leadership. You can adopt this unique perspective or internal dialogue for making a difference, if you really choose to change your personality and behaviors. At any given moment in time, you can make a conscious decision to take your life and leadership to a more meaningful level; you can decide *right now* to re-examine your personal effectiveness and commit to doing what it will take to become the person you want to be, capable of influencing others in a desired and good direction. Zing! has many benefits. Do any, or all, of the following appeal to you?

Take good relationships and make them great;
Create opportunities for others to connect;
Accomplish goals more efficiently;
Recruit involvement and support in a particular organization;
Inspire others to be more productive;
Establish and build new relationships;
Serve as a role model or mentor to inspire others;
Greater ease initiating conversations with strangers;
Enhanced ability to facilitate connections;
Put self in greater positions of opportunity; and/or
Enhanced happiness.

Chapter 2

HAPPINESS MATTERS

*"I believe that the rendering of useful service is
the common duty of mankind and that only in the purifying
fire of sacrifice is the dross of selfishnessconsumed and the
greatness of the human soul set free."*
- John D. Rockefeller, Jr.

At the end of the day, are you happy? Is your very soul set free? You can't ignore this question because you don't like the answer. Happiness matters. More specifically, your happiness should matter to you. Despite all the self-help or leadership development books written (including this one) there really isn't anything complicated about finding the "secret to success," "meaning of life" or "path to happiness." The answer to all three familiar questions is so simple it consistently gets dismissed: Serve others and you end up serving yourself! In other words, happiness comes to those who bring happiness to others.

What makes you happy? Knowing specifically what you are looking for makes it easier to find. Have you ever wondered, for instance, when a dog chases a car down the street, what exactly the dog plans to do once it "catches" it? What are you chasing? Many believe things (i.e. "stuff") bring happiness – a new car, bigger house, latest iPhone, or a dozen Krispy Kreme donuts. Some believe power, promotion or social status bring happiness. Then there are those who believe they would be happy if they'd just meet the right person, lose ten pounds or pass a particular course in college!

I know people who have all these things and more, yet they still seek more. They aren't content with what they have accomplished, possess or have become. Their lives lack real meaning because they are in search of something that isn't real in the first place; the belief that happiness *follows* instead of *proceeds* all that is worth having. This lesson I thankfully learned in my early thirties (yet wish I'd learned in my twenties) when I was trying to live everyone else's definition of "having it all" and woke up one day with the realization: I have two beautiful infants, a wonderful husband, and successful career yet in truth, I can't do it all! To say I was merely "going through the motions" is an understatement. On the outside I was functioning, but on the inside, I was miserable. It was as if I'd gotten on a merry-go-round and couldn't get off. Despite achieving what I thought I wanted, when I got it, I wasn't happy – I was a certifiable nutcase. It took me awhile to realize the problem: I was making a living, but I wasn't making a life.

The ability to do what you want to do is the purest form of truth. If you aren't searching for truth, then you aren't seeking happiness. There's no point in continuing to read this book if happiness isn't important to you, or you prefer to play the martyr, stay miserable, live a beige existence, waste your talents, and make the people around you miserable! You will never have Zing! if you lead a hypocritical life. You will never have followers if people doubt the sincerity of your direction or question your motives. Your leadership isn't possible without your life. The desire to reach your fullest potential in *both* your life and leadership matters. When you have achieved this sense of applied integrity, you have achieved truth.

You clearly want something. Is it happiness, contentment, internal peace, personal growth, or to feel alive again – or, the permission to seek these things? There's nothing wrong with admitting you find yourself in a place of wanting change, or wanting more. In fact, there's a lot right with knowing you were meant to do great things and need to hold yourself to higher expectations. Your source of internal disturbance or "chaos of character" is allowing you to realize something isn't as it should be. You can dwell on the *why not* or you can focus on the *what's next?* You get to direct the life you live by making choices and taking back control over your destiny. When you adopt the proper attitude (i.e. Zing!) everything else just falls into place.

Requirements for Happiness

There are three essential internal conditions necessary for achieving happiness. At times having two out of the three can sustain you, at times having just one does the trick. Having all three reduces the frequency of having to "fake it until you make it!" When you radiate a genuine sense of happiness and optimism you position yourself to say and do things resulting in the outcome you desire. The degree to which you will become a person of Zing! is contingent upon the degree to which you buy into the *Zing! Philosophy*: The energy you put out there is the energy you get to draw from! Positive energy leads to good things happening.

Condition One: Having control over your life.

Doing what it takes to manage your time in a manner consistent with your priorities is challenging at best. However, it is essential in feeling the necessary control over your destiny.

When someone or something dictates your decision making and you are not a willing participant, it's up to you to first identify the "controllers" and dismantle them. You are a willing party until you decide to take back ownership of your present, and thus, your future! When you sense or suspect something needs to change, or is turning into a potential obstacle to overcome, be a grown up. Acknowledge you aren't as competent as you should be, for example, and start working on being more competent!

One reason you might not have been working on bringing Zing! into your life and leadership until now is you literally hadn't thought about it; never crossed your mind that you were being held back due to a lack of this significant approach. In *Reawakening Your Passion for Work*, Richard Boyatiz, Annie McKee, and Daniel Goleman identify six "trigger" phrases clearly signaling it's time to make necessary changes in your life. Have you spoken any of the following phrases lately?

> *"I feel trapped."*
> *"I'm bored."*
> *"I'm not the person I want to be."*
> *"I won't compromise my ethics."*
> *"I can't ignore the call."*
> *"Life is too short."*

Think about some of the more frustrating situations you've found yourself in recently. If you had been better able to override competing forces (i.e. boss' temper, colleague's competitiveness, daughter's teenage rebellion, and so on) to positively influence others, would you have produced a more desirable outcome? In addition to the list of six trigger phrases above, consider your "internal talk." Have you thought any of the following thoughts lately?

> *I don't have any close friends.*
> *I don't like the friends I do have.*

My dog won't play with me.
I feel old.
People don't seem to notice me.
I feel unappreciated.
People around me are happier than I am.
I don't look my best.
I find little enjoyment in what I do on a daily basis.
There's always tomorrow.
I used to be fun to be around.
Why does this always happen to me?
Whatever.

Once you've accepted you need to change it up, doing what it takes isn't as hard as you think. For example, if you dislike your major course of study, change majors. If your significant other puts you on an "allowance," tells you what to wear, or intimidates you into submission, respect yourself enough to end the relationship. If your children tell you what to do, treat you with disrespect, or feel "entitled" to have things you can't afford to provide for them, look in the mirror and repeat until you believe it, "I am the parent, they are the children!" When your boss continually stifles your creativity, prevents you from advancing, or consistently takes credit for your work, give yourself credit for having a brain in your head and start looking for another job!

Be willing to admit you'd like it if things were different then identify what things. Put it all on the table! Whether issues around your weight, fitness, quality of relationships, job satisfaction, ability to advance, influence on those you employ, recreational pursuits, and so on, work to identify where you feel out of control. You can't change what you can't identify. Be specific! Start now.

Exploration: Something Needs to Change

Directions: Make a list of the ten things you wish you had more control over in your life. Ask yourself, "Where is their inconsistency between what I want to be doing and what I am doing?"

1. _____
2. _____
3. _____
4. _____
5. _____
6. _____
7. _____
8. _____
9. _____
10. _____

Condition Two: Count your blessings on a daily basis.

I'm always fascinated (and humbled) to watch news broadcasts depicting the enormous appreciation shown by those with so little who just received a few new books or a pair of sneakers. It continues to boggle my mind that the highest percentage of contributors to charities in the United States come from the lowest income brackets. Yet it all makes sense: When you have very little, you understand what it is like to want for something, so you give what you can. Likewise, when you barely have the necessities of life, it seems irrational to the point of ridiculousness, to get caught up in materialistic pursuits.

The ability to be sincerely thankful for all you've received in your life is a gift. There is great power in this gift because it forces you to literally stop long enough to take inventory of all you have, as opposed to, all that's not there or wrong. On a daily basis, being able to notice the small gestures, amount of opportunity you've been afforded and the beauty around you, will free (or lift) the negative forces of never "having enough."

Instead of always asking, "What can I get?" come from a perspective of plenty and ask, "What can I give?" This approach is basic to achieving Zing! and returns the favor.

To literally take a step in the right direction, when your feet hit the floor in the morning – or upon your rising, simply say out loud, "Thank you." When you see someone who consistently does something for you (despite being paid to do it) go out of your way to pay them a compliment. Before you put any nourishment in your mouth, stop and show gratitude. Being appreciative for even the smallest sources of joy, basic living needs and support allows you to practice the skill of gratitude – a skill that suppresses the more reinforced societal mindsets of entitlement, possessiveness, supersized, selfishness, and feel good materialism.

What are the blessings in your life? Say those most obvious out loud, but reserve the space below for those offerings which you sometimes forget to acknowledge, or don't always view as a plus. Just because you don't like your job, doesn't mean you can't be thankful you have a source of income until you find something better. Just because the high cost of college is causing you to work while you also try to be a student, doesn't mean you can't be thankful for the opportunity to get an education. Just because you bought this book to enhance your ability to influence, doesn't mean you can't be appreciative of those who have challenged you to work harder, care deeper and reach higher!

Exploration: Blessings Overlooked

Directions: Take inventory of those things, opportunities and people in your world – past and present, that have gotten you this far. Focus on the daily blessings, regardless of how small, and say the more obvious ones out loud. Your goal is to pay better attention to the volume of your blessings.

1. _____
2. _____
3. _____
4. _____
5. _____
6. _____
7. _____
8. _____
9. _____
10. _____

Condition Three: Making a difference.

Knowing your existence on this planet matters is powerful. When you sit down at the end of the day and know your work has allowed someone else to do their work, you've made a difference; when you know in your heart, the compliment you've paid a child built their self-esteem, you've made a difference; and when you feel you've added to a classroom discussion, made someone laugh, or helped someone through an illness, you've made a difference. The internal dilemma arises when in *your* opinion, what you do on a daily basis doesn't matter anymore. Your work or efforts don't add meaning to your life, nor do you believe anyone else benefits. This is a judgment call *you* make about *your* very existence – It's *your* call. You can't be "talked into" feeling better about how you are spending your time if according to your morals and values (or after you get Zing!) it's not consistent with how you want to conduct your life or how you choose to leave your fingerprints on the world.

You can, however, re-think your potential contributions as you soul search. You can look at how you are spending your time, make adjustments and start replacing the less meaningful things with the more meaningful pursuits. At some point in your life *you* must grow up and stop majoring in the minors! You will have to ask yourself the tough questions (many of which are posed in the chapters to follow) and decide how to proceed.

The most achieving people in the world continually ask themselves, "What's next?" when they arrive to a place they once set as a goal. Sometimes in life, you just don't know where you are until you get there! Give yourself latitude to grow, adjust and re-invent yourself. Although you can (are encouraged to) solicit and consider what others may think, it's not their life. If you don't see your existence as significant, you have no choice but to rely on external sources of motivation (like a pay check, ability to put your children through college, or being appreciated by those around you) instead of the more natural internal sources which go wherever you go!

Exploration: The Tough Questions

Directions: Read through the questions below. Spend time reflecting upon the meaning for the question before you answer it. Copy the questions onto a 3x5 card which sting the hardest, or are most difficult to answer, and reflect upon them in the weeks ahead.

When is your personality the most transparent?
When you were a teenager, what did you think would define your "success?"
How well do people who know you, really know you?
If the world ended tomorrow, who would you be most proud of?
What is the proudest day in your life?
When you are "at your best" what are you doing?
What does it feel like to know "victory?"
If your life ended tomorrow, what would be your legacy?
What do you want your life to say to others?
In a world free from responsibility, what would you be doing?

After exploring the above questions, return to the most important three repeated below and simply answer YES or NO:

Do I feel as if I have control over your life? _____
On a consistent basis, do I count my blessings? _____
Does my life have meaning? _____

The Role of Zing!

When you make a difference in someone else's life, your life will be forever different. You might know what will enhance your happiness, yet not feel worthy of doing what it takes to be happy. Believe you deserve what you want. Believe in your decision making power and that your life has purpose, even if don't know the specifics. Purpose has a funny way of revealing itself to you when you least expect it. This belief allows you to optimistically and freely move forward releasing the energy that either pulls others towards you – or pushes them away. Every moment that passes is an opportunity for you to create or be created, influence or follow, make a decision or do nothing (which is technically a decision) with the potential to drastically change your destiny. Choose to be happy. Let your life and leadership speak!

Chapter 3

LIFE AND LEADERSHIP

"Success is the maximum utilization of the ability you have."
- Zig Ziglar

In short, I'm short. I'm always going to be short. In fact, I'll probably only get shorter. I can't change this fact of nature. I can, however, request a wireless microphone before I speak so I don't have to stand behind a podium and look like a talking nose. I can stay fit so I stand vertically, not horizontally. After being introduced at social functions, I can ask the taller guests to sit at a table with me (so that my neck doesn't break during a fifteen-minute conversation.) I have learned how to work with what I've got so I can get what I want – that is, to make a difference! I've also learned that life and leadership go hand and hand; you don't get one without the other.

Every life is meant to lead. People aren't born into roles of greatness; they become great because there is a need – whether personal, societal, emotional, environmental or cultural. Technically, Hitler was a phenomenal leader – if you define a leader as someone who can influence others to do whatever he/she wants them to do regardless if it's evil or dark. Making a difference is making the *right* difference. Your motives matter. Good intentions live behind the actions of influential leaders. Whether building houses for senior citizens, planning youth mission trips, owning a general store, heading up a construction company, or being a director of admissions at a school for learning disabled children; when your efforts result in a greater good and you know this to be true, you make a difference. You *are* a leader.

The majority of educators I am blessed to know teach because they want their students to learn. It's not about the money; it's about making a difference. Conversely, just because someone makes a lot of money doesn't mean they aren't capable of serving a greater good. Just because they devote the majority of their time and talents to building a corporation doesn't mean they aren't concerned about the future. And, hopefully, just because someone sits in the very front of the plane doesn't automatically mean they will take their shoes off, or be insulting to your child. Senior researcher at Yale Law School, former president of Connecticut College, and author of *The Greater Good* Claire Gaudiani states, "It's not that Americans have been generous because we're rich, we're rich because we have been generous." Her research confirms both the visible and invisible impact of philanthropy in America. My rule: It doesn't matter how much money you make; it matters what you do with the money you've got!

Defining Leadership

Leadership is how things change not what you wear. You don't put "it" on in the morning, like a tie, and take "it" off at night. One of America's greatest leadership scholars John W. Gardner offers: "Leadership is the process of *persuasion* or example by which an individual (or leadership team) induces a group to pursue objectives held by the leader or shared by the leader and his or her followers." Your goal as leader is to *inspire* others to action. Another great leadership educator Dr. John C. Maxwell confirms: "Leadership is influence-nothing more, nothing less."

Understanding how to lead effectively requires you to embrace a definition of leadership most aliened with your principles, morals and values. The Zing! approach is reflective of definitions (like those above) where the outcome of a *process* is service to mankind. Respected leadership icon Robert Greenleaf believes: "The great leader is seen as servant first, and that simple fact is the key to [the leader's] greatness." Servant leadership is neither a new concept nor one to risk extinction. In their most recent book *A Leader's Legacy*, James M. Kouzes and Barry Z. Posner build upon this premise by claiming "leaders will not be remembered for what they do for themselves, rather for what they do for others." Widely referenced in higher education, Susan R. Komives, Nance Lucas and Timothy R. McMahon, authors of *Exploring Leadership: For College Students Who Want to Make a Difference,* define leadership as "a relational and ethical process of people together attempting to accomplish positive change."

All these definitions place great significance on the person as leader – not the position. You can have the titles, a corner office, and diplomas on your walls, but if you aren't a decent human being concerned about making a positive contribution in the world, you aren't a leader. Positions and titles are often the very things preventing you from doing what truly matters; they can restrict your freedom to be creative, require you to spend valuable time and resources fighting off negative influences; and hold you contractually to carrying out someone else's mission as opposed to your own. Just because you are in the "position" of head delegate, representative, president, manager, teacher, or student doesn't necessarily make you a person of influence – or a leader – in other's minds.

In Search of a Leader
Author Unknown

I went on search to become a leader. I searched high and low. I spoke with authority. People listened...

I sought to inspire confidence, but the crowd responded, "Why should I trust you?" I postured, and I assumed the look of leadership with a countenance that flowed with confidence and pride. But many passed me by and never noticed my air of elegance. I ran ahead of the others, pointed the way to new heights. I demonstrated that I knew the route to greatness. And then I looked back and I was alone.

"What shall I do?" I queried. "I've tried hard and used all that I know." And I sat down and pondered long. And then I listened to the voices around me... and I heard what the group was trying to accomplish. I rolled up my sleeves and joined in the work. As we worked, I asked, "Are we all together in what we want to do and how to get the job done?" We thought together, and we fought together, and we struggled towards our goal.

I found myself encouraging the fainthearted. I sought the ideas of those too shy to speak out. I taught those who had little skill. I praised those who worked hard. When our task was completed, one of the group turned to me and said, "This would not have been done but for your leadership." At first I said, "I didn't lead. I just worked with the rest."
And then I understood - leadership is not a goal. Leadership is a way of reaching a goal.

With your enhanced understanding of leadership as "a process of using your presence to positively influence others," comes the very real question: "Do you have what it takes?"

Chapter 4

LEADERSHIP IS RELATIONAL

"A loyal constituency is won when people, consciously or otherwise, judge the leader to be capable of solving their problems and meeting their needs."
- John W. Gardner

One way to explain how you view leadership is to ask: Are you among those of us who can be alone in a room and crack ourselves up? If your answer is "Yes," does that mean you really *are* all that funny to others? Because Zing! is rooted in a combination of leadership models, including transformational leadership (or charismatic models of leadership) you can't dismiss the role of *reverence* or *relationships based upon awe* in place of the more outdated concept of blind submission. Leading and living with Zing! is a result of your positive influence on others; making it impossible to lead from a point of isolation, solitude or strict authority. You can't technically consider yourself a "crack up" if you are the only one who ever laughs at your jokes or in your presence!

Your opinion of your influence is just that – *your* opinion. Because leadership is relational in nature, determining whether or not you are being influential (or possess the appropriate attitudes, characteristics and actions,) requires interaction, immersion and contact with other people. It's *their* reaction to your presence that indicates your success or failure as a person of influence. You can say, "I'm a teacher," but if no one learns because of your abilities (or lack thereof) – are you really helping students learn? It's one thing to say, "I'm a leader," but if nothing or anyone changes for the better because of your efforts (or lack thereof) – are you really making a difference?

The instrument created to measure your Zing! potential is called the Inventory of Influence and is found in Appendix A. The inventory has two distinct columns; one for your opinion, but more importantly, one for someone who interacts with you because it is *their* opinion on how often you engage in specific attributes of influence which accurately reveals your charismatic impact, or influence on them. One size doesn't fit all. You can take the inventory as often as needed. This allows you to measure your growth in specific areas and continually learn how you are being perceived by others.

The most effective leaders are connectors and relationship builders. They don't operate from a corner office dictating or delegating in a downward fashion void of interaction. They pay attention to how they are perceived, observe communication styles, and actively study the complexity of human behavior. They seek feedback, evaluation from those around them, and opportunities to better understand how they are being perceived by others.

The State of Massachusetts elected its first Afro-American governor in 2006. He was significantly outspent in the election and had never held a highly visible political office like his "shoe in" opponent who was the current Lieutenant Governor. He ran a "grass roots" campaign and instead of television ads, he went door to door, held community meetings and focused on people over politics. He didn't engage in negative campaigning, instead choosing to run on the slogan, "Together We Can!" This effectively summarized the leadership vision of Governor Deval Patrick who understood the value in having an honest assessment of how he was being perceived.

To improve upon your Zing! potential you can't avoid evaluation, assessment or tough conversations. You will have to become comfortable with soliciting and receiving others' opinions about you without lashing back at the brave souls who risked being honest! The more opinions you get, the more accurate the information you will collect about the correlation between your *perceived* and *apparent* influence on those you seek to lead – or be around including: family members, neighbors, supervisors, employees, classmates, teachers and so on. You can and should discover who you are in the eyes of others in a variety of ways. Which of the following methods of collecting feedback are you willing to use?

Methods of Soliciting Feedback:
- Copy the Inventory of Influence (Found in Appendix A) and give it to those you interact with;
- Make up a "survey" where personal questions are mixed in with less personal ones;
- Use www.SurveyMonkey.com to distribute your survey;
- Take people you associate with to lunch and directly ask them to "rate" you on a few personal questions;
- Ask someone who knows you well to actively seek other's opinions about how you interact with them and the quality of the interactions;
- Record interactions you have with one person over the course of a week or month in a journal, then give

the journal to someone you trust who can interpret what the other person most likely "heard" during your conversations;

- Simply ask random people you come into contact with, "Would you mind telling me what first impression did I give you?"

Mistaken Identity

My son Jake and I went to Washington, D.C. for his tenth birthday. While boarding the plane, I reminded him of proper plane etiquette. Apparently, I had made my point relatively early in our conversation, because as I began to open my mouth on our way down the jet way, he commented, "I get it already." Enjoying the frequent flyer perks, we were the first to board the plane and find our upgraded seats in the First Class cabin. Jake's backpack was rather well-stuffed and he was having difficulty storing it in the overhead bin.

As he struggled, other First Class passengers boarded and quickly became frustrated at having to wait while my son fiddled with his backpack. Waiting to take their seats did not prevent them, however, from commenting to the parties on their cell phones about the delay Jake was causing them. Within earshot one man said, "I'll be in my seat as soon as this little kid gets his act together... he should be in coach, anyway." Jake quickly pulled down his backpack and stepped away from the aisle. At this point, and as though their rudeness had earned them the right, they completely stuffed the exact bin my son was attempting to use with their own luggage!

We were dumbfounded. Together, we stuffed his bag under the seat in front of us, leaving him with no leg room. I leaned over and said quietly, "Hey, Birthday Boy, always remember this: just because you sit in First Class, doesn't mean you are first class." (I resisted the temptation to say it louder.)

Chapter 5

INFLUENCE AND FOLLOWSHIP

"To live is so startling it leaves little time for anything else."
- Emily Dickinson

Have you ever been persuaded or positively influenced by bad ideas delivered well – or, great ideas delivered poorly? Have you willingly followed those who intentionally and transparently set out to serve only themselves, but you liked where they were going? Do you find yourself trusting someone who lies, cheats and is deceitful because you live by the motto: People are inherently good? Understanding the psychology of influence is difficult because it's so personal. It's often hard to explain why you like someone yet dislike another; or why someone likes you and not your friends. What makes the connection for one person is not necessarily what will work for another, yet certain commonalities exist which provide a useful foundation for our discussion.

To make this point, think back for a moment to the one individual who intentionally set out to make you a better person. How did they accomplish their goal? How did he/she leave their legacy on you? You might not have appreciated their attempt to make you a better person, bring an observation of your behavior to your attention, or interfere with the direction of your life, but through their presence and persistence you changed for the better. You were on the receiving end of someone's Zing! and consequently, experienced positive growth and development.

Exploration: The Circles of Zing!

Directions: On a blank sheet of paper, draw a one inch in diameter circle in the center. Place eight similar circles about three inches from the center circle on the paper, and then connect each circle to the center one with a line. You should see something resembling either the Solar System if you are a Right Brained individual, or wheel of a bicycle if you are a Left Brained individual. Place your name in the center circle. Place the names of people in your life that *intentionally* changed you with their Zing! appeal. On one side of the line going from you to them, identify how they accomplished this feat; on the bottom side of the line identify what obstacle or challenge they had to overcome to do so! Add more circles if you need them.

These are the Zing! people in your life; each had to overcome different obstacles and each used a different means of reaching you proving the tricky nature of well placed intentions. You may unconsciously influence others when you least expect it, or intentionally set out to leave a positive set of fingerprints on someone or something using a well planned out strategy! You don't always choose when you leave a legacy. The list below suggests only a few of the ways people become recipients of your Zing! – or are touched by your life and leadership.

How Influence Happens:
- Through a direct conversation rooted in love;
- By receiving a performance evaluation;
- When they observe the positive outcomes of your behavior;

- By having opportunities either taken away or offered;
- Through working side by side;
- By positive reinforcement of "better" behaviors;
- When included in decisions affecting their life;
- By being asked to participate;
- Through direct challenge or confrontation;
- When disappointment doesn't become dislike;
- By overhearing conversations or reading something about them;

People with Zing! understand human behavior. They are students of the most difficult and hardest subjects of all – leadership and life. Ironically referred to as "soft skills," the command of this subject matter requires perceptiveness, intuitiveness, empathy, interpretation, and the rare ability to go from "theory to practice." Knowing *how* to persuade, inspire, empower, excite, influence, mentor, support, be likeable, and "read" someone's intentions, for instance, is a skill set worthy of advanced degrees, research and higher learning. You can know *about* these talents, but that won't guarantee you can *apply* them; the potential consequence of this irony is the belief you are being followed because of your extraordinary ability to lead when in fact, your followers have their own motivation – little of which has to do with you! As you move to the front row in Psychology of Followership 101, consider how your relationship with specific individuals is explained by any of these considerations:

- *People want to feel important and visible – like they matter.*
- *People are impressed by those who appear prepared and well rehearsed.*
- *People look favorably on those who clearly show consideration for others.*
- *People connect with those who make them laugh and feel good about themselves.*
- *People will get behind ideas they help to formulate.*

- *People long to have faith in those who are trustworthy.*
- *People respond more favorably to optimism than gloom and doom.*
- *People respect those who have accomplished something remarkable.*
- *People admire someone who overcomes in the face of adversity.*
- *People like to feel safe.*
- *People will hold those who are consistently competent yet humble in high esteem.*
- *People are social creatures who value being included.*
- *People will support who or what helps them to achieve and thus, support their own goals.*

Maxwell's Model of Followship

Dr. John C. Maxwell's perspectives on leadership have greatly influenced my work. We share the belief: Leadership is influence – nothing more and nothing less. Maxwell offers a "user-friendly" model for understanding how all of the above conditions come together and make sense. Through his *Model of Followship* he explains leadership from the perspective of those you are wanting to influence, or change through your presence, by encouraging the leader's exploration of how his/her potential followers would answer the question: Why should I follow you or permit myself to be influenced by you? Maxwell concludes there are five distinct reasons why individuals are motivated to follow someone:

POSITION:

The most basic level someone will follow your lead is because they have to follow or see following you as a means to getting what they want and need (like a paycheck.) You hold a position of "authority" over them and they have a duty or responsibility to do what you ask them to do.

PERMISSION:

The next level suggests people will turn over some degree of self regulation and allow you to lead them is because it's easier than having to take the lead themselves, think on their own, or be responsible for the outcomes. You are viewed as capable, or a more convenient choice to direct an organization, activity or project, which is totally acceptable to them.

PRODUCTION:

In this middle level, true leadership emerges as you are respected for your commitment to the organization or cause and are believed to have only good intentions. Because of the desires of members to be a part of the organization and have it succeed, you have influence to the extent you will make the organization achieve its goals.

PEOPLE DEVELOPMENT:

Building upon the more personal needs of members, in this level your Zing! appeal emerges because you are connecting to the individual needs of members. They see you as being not only committed to the organization, but to them personally; you are perceived to be helping them grow, accomplish their goals, and achieve. They follow you because of what you have done for them on a personal level.

PERSONHOOD:

This is a level very few leaders reach because you have to be seen as an individual of exemplary character, ideas, accomplishment, vision, integrity and influence. Members follow you - whether you are in personal contact with them or not - because they perceive you to be extraordinary!

Impressive Characteristics of Leaders

Like Zing!, Maxwell's model is also based upon growing reverence and the belief we more joyfully follow those we are inspired to follow, not required to follow. As human beings we are naturally drawn to energy greater than our own, and to constructive forces or admirable missions. We allow ourselves to be guided by those who give us faith and appear able to achieve their missions. We are impressed by unwavering integrity, a willingness to take on causes larger than ourselves and the humble – yet, so powerful servants, like Mother Teresa, Nelson Mandela, Eleanor Roosevelt, and Frederick Douglass, for example.

We are impressed by those who have found unconventional ways to achieve unimaginable goals, like the more contemporary examples of Bill Gate's and Ted Turner's efforts to immunize Third World countries; Lance Armstrong's push to raise money for cancer research through increasing the quantity of awareness and value in smaller acts of financial support; Oprah's efforts to build better schools in South Africa; Michael J. Fox's efforts to increase the research activity around a cure for neuro-muscular diseases; and Al Gore's efforts to educate the world on the real threat of global warming.

Although impressive, the greatest sources of inspiration aren't celebrities and national figures – they are positive influences in our immediate and daily surroundings. Former President William Jefferson Clinton in his most recent book, *Giving: How Each of Us Can Change the World* writes: "We all have the capacity to do great things." He offers examples of innovative and exceptional effort of every day people from all walks of life who are actively engaged in service and leading by example. When the results of your efforts are there for you to observe, the impact on your life is tremendous. You work harder to become a good teacher when you watch the child next door skip to school every day because her teacher makes her feel good about herself; you reach out to a stranger because you've watched your local pastor treat everyone he meets with unconditional positive regard; you study harder for your next exam because your roommate takes her academics much more seriously than you do and it appears to result in higher grades; and, because of what you "live," you become a Big Sister as part of the Big Brother Big Sister program because your professor brought his "little brother" to class one day and the way that child clearly admired his "big brother" is imprinted in head.

Likability and Influence

Finally, whether or not someone "likes" you as a person, may play a role in your ability to positively influence them. It's easier to do things for people we genuinely like versus those who are irritating. Your *likeability factor* will either open doors for you to follow, or shut them before you've said, "Hello." There is value in being a nice person and showing kindness to others on many levels. Depending on your mission, however, being liked may be the least of your worries. You are engaged in a vision where their will be considerable opposition, defensiveness and resistance; being liked is an unrealistic expectation. True leaders often have to accept the fact: Leadership isn't a popularity contest.

When it does matter whether or not you are perceived as "likeable," you will be more effective if you do care what others think! In *A Leader's Legacy*, Kouzes and Posner, write, "Leadership is a relationship between those who aspire to lead and those who choose to follow" and predict the quality of your relationships will determine your legacy. It is their contention leaders should want to be liked and should care about putting forth the effort and understanding to build healthy relationships. Part of this understanding is accepting what others want to know *about* you before they will follow! They offer the following six considerations:

What are your values, beliefs, aspirations and dreams?
Who has influenced you the most?
What prepares you for the job you're doing.
What you're like as a person.
What drives you?
What are your hobbies and other personal tidbits?

Chapter 6

THE CHARISMA CONNECTION

"Don't mis-underestimate me!"
- Former President of the Free World

L ast but not least; the exploration of charisma as it relates to your ability to Zing! and arrive at different place than you began. As with previous notions of influence, followship, and likeability, *charisma* is a function of how others view you, *not* how you view yourself. Harvard University anthropologist Charles Lindholm, as quoted in *Charisma* by Dr. Tony Alessandra, states: "charisma can be revealed only in interaction with others." It is a multi-dimensional construct requiring another force (could that be Zing!?) to be present so the stronger influence can be exerted against the weaker force. To be more charismatic involves connecting to others on a variety of levels, including intellectual, emotional, spiritual, and physical.

Charisma is an "idea" we form about someone; the person we *believe* and often *need* them to be. What once was a rather clear and rarely debated phenomenon for centuries, now finds itself open to many interpretations, applications and definitions. Whether you call charisma "it" or "Zing!" or use it interchangeably with terms like *influence, personal magnetism* and *likeability,* the phenomenon is one of "interpretation" or "perception." Organizational behaviorist Rakesh Khurana suggests that since its adaptation from Christian theology, *charisma* has evolved to mean a "set of personal qualities that inspire awe and submission in others." After considerable study, he concludes: "...charisma remains as difficult to define as art or love. Few who advocate it are able to convey what they mean by the term."[1] I believe the term will continue to evolve as the world's needs for positive and influential leadership evolves.

The Origin of Charisma

The word *charisma* is derived from the ancient Greek word *charms* meaning "gift or favor." When it was adopted by Christian churches, it was used to describe gifts or "charismata" from God and associated with individuals who carried out extraordinary feats like healing the sick or prophecy. The apostle Paul used *charms* in the New Testament when speaking of church leaders and other disciples who possess the "gifts of the Holy Spirit." As noted by Khurana, "according to Paul, those gifted with charisma included 'good leaders'. . . [and] church members with extraordinary endowments, such as the power to speak in tongues or work miracles."[2] The use or application of the term, to secular leadership didn't occur until the 20th century when German sociologist Max Weber used it as a way to describe one of the forces of authority in society. Weber determined "charismatic authority" did rely on laws, rules, positions or titles, but rather from how the individual's character was able to impact forces of change and innovation. He believed charismatic authority came from a faith in the charismatic's exemplary character.

The Changing Meaning of Charisma

The nature and meaning of charisma has changed over time for a variety of reasons. First and foremost, the negative backlash of corporate scandals involving flashy CEO corporate superstars (or crooks) makes it necessary to question in this day and age whether it's good or bad to be a "charismatic leader." Secondly, most Americans are discovering that despite corporate leaders' high levels of competency, we cannot realistically assume that one person can make or break an entire corporation. This assumption ignores the significant role of domestic and global forces – especially terrorist attacks, stock market drops, and war. Rudolph Guiliani, wasn't even viewed as a charismatic leader until *after* September 11, 2001. Previously, he had to overcome bad publicity from a very public divorce and was known for his "tough" style of leadership, especially regarding crime and law enforcement.

The Superstars of Charismatic Leadership

One of the first leaders to fit the more contemporary "CEO Superstar" application of charisma was Lee Iaccoca, former chairman of the Chrysler Corporation. Unlike many of his modern counterparts, he moved up through the ranks of the same company he eventually headed. Today, many "charismatic superstars" are transplanted from other organizations, never having paid their dues in the dynasty they now control. Although a shift is taking place, a degree of celebrity is still associated with, and expected from, a majority of today's high-powered, high-profile corporate leaders. It's not uncommon to see their faces on the cover of *Newsweek, The Wall Street Journal*, and *People*.

Charismatic icons of the Modern Era also include: great orators like Elizabeth Dole, Dr. Martin Luther King Jr., and Winston Churchill; corporate icons, like Jack Welch of General Electric, Carly Fiorina of Hewlett-Packard, David Stern of the National Basketball Association, and Oprah Winfrey of Harpo Productions; professional athletes like, Tiger Woods, Mia Hamm, Lance Armstrong and Andre Agassi; television personalities like, Dr. Phil, Matt Lauer, Katie Couric and Jon Sterwart; and entertainers like Ellen DeGeneres, Madonna, and Bono. These are the images that might pop immediately into your thoughts when you see the word "charisma."

Over the past ten years, however, there has been a noticeable shift to a more informal and less significant use of the "charisma" to describe individuals without any corporate connection or celebrity. The appeal of this more casual application includes being able to identify individuals literally within our reach, instead of admiring from a far! Declining numbers of impressive national figures truly void of scandal, over exposure, and [you fill in the blank] are causing those of us normally tempted to be impressed, to be just the opposite.

"Charisma" has become a term to characterize a more natural magnetic force, image or personality that's too complicated to describe trait by trait, but summed up with "charisma." Being able to say someone has "it" or "that thing" or "charisma" takes much less effort, yet gets the point across. Applied to children, grandparents, students, teachers, and other every day people, "charisma" has become an adjective, adverb and noun – almost a by-product of someone's influence as opposed to the cause of it. Do you have charisma, and if so, is there proof?

Measuring Influence

Leading edge research on measuring transformational leadership or charismatic leadership, conducted by Conger, Kanungo, Menon and Mathur (1997) proved valuable in my search to find a way of measuring potential influence – or Zing! because they were able to identify traits of "successful charismatic leaders" based upon three dependent factors:

follower's reverence, sense of group identity and perceived group task performance.₃ They found the following five characteristics as deemed by their subordinates to significantly correlate with the desired outcomes of managers:

Possess a unique strategic vision;
Show sensitivity to their member's needs;
Show sensitivity to the environment;
Engage in unconventional behavior; and
Willingness to take risks.

After additional research, the original tool used to measure these attributes was found to be psychometrically sound. The tool is a twenty item questionnaire called the C-K Scale (Conger-Kanungo Scale) and despite being met with great skepticism, has been found to be a valid and reliable measure of charismatic aptitude. Respecting the practical application of their findings and ability to measure charismatic potential, the Inventory of Influence (Appendix A) was created. This assessment also relies on other's opinions of your attributes based upon the frequency or regularity of these behaviors in context with the person doing the assessment. The inventory operationalizes the five charismatic characteristics identified above into 40 items which include those conversely reflected negative attributes referred to as *Individual Detractors* (introduced in Chapter 8.)

Chapter 7

ZING! IT ON

*"One can never consent to creep
when one feels an impulse to soar."*
- Helen Keller

Have you ever been a chaperone? It's an adventure. I think chaperones need other chaperones. On a four-day camping trip with my son's fourth grade class, I learned two things I'll never forget. Number one: Children *can* be taught to take only what they can eat. Number two: Parents should not be left unattended.

How did the first amazing feat occur? Given all the reasons *why not* and all the collective skepticism of my parental peers, the camp counselors were presented with more than enough obstacles to overcome to teach children (and adults) how to decrease wasted food. They were successful for a variety of reasons: presentation of a united front, faith in the participants, creative approach clearly communicated, previous success, valid means of measuring "success" and a well defined plan!

The hypothesis: As tables of campers compete to have the lowest number of pounds of left-over food, the total amount of wasted food in the room will go down. Additional incentive was provided in the form of a camp song during the ritual of weighing the leftover food. I've conveniently forgotten it.

In theory, the success of reducing wasteful eating behaviors is a direct result of each consumer knowing in advance the role he or she plays in the total score. Aside from parents hiding unused apples down their shirts, the children made a remarkable discovery in four short days. They learned an important lesson about world hunger while being fed. They learned how one person makes a difference. All they needed for this lesson was a set of rules (or perspective), a scale, and a song. They achieved a greater social good because counselors with Zing! took the time to "set the stage."

What is it you need to begin? Just because you *say* you want what being more appealing, confident and charismatic can get you, does that mean you *are willing* to go through the time and trouble to focus on personal growth and development? It's often easier to identify and discuss someone else's weaknesses, for instance, than our own! Moving forward requires strategies of internal motivation. It also requires some guidelines, a set of directions and possibly a song. Understanding the process of change will also assist you putting to practice the 21 Insights introduced in the next chapter.

People change for different reasons; some because they will literally die if they don't change. Others change for the fun of it; they try a different hair style, drive to work a different way every day or never go to the same restaurant twice. Then there are those who change because they don't have a choice. There are no real consequences to their actions, and inactions. As suggested in our discussion on happiness, if nothing changes, nothing changes. You won't know how to Zing! if you don't intentionally start altering your attitudes, perceptions and behaviors now. The lesson you will learn: If you fail to act, you've guaranteed you won't succeed.

The Principles of Zing!

Principal One: *Zing! is energy and movement translated into specific actions or skills which are learnable by anyone who wants to "kick it up a notch" and become more influential.*

You learned how to ride a bike, shampoo your hair and tie your shoes – all when you were developmentally ready to do so. There are prescribed ages when you were "supposed" to learn these things. Maybe you were a few months early or late in your mastering of these skills; eventually, you were developmentally ready and didn't have to think about how to ride a bike, shampoo your hair, or tie your shoes – you just did! From the mastering of these skills, you were able to do more and learn more; not only because of your new competencies, but because of the boost to your confidence and self-esteem. Success leads to success.

Like riding a bike, shampooing your hair or tying your shoes, Zing! is the skill of knowing: The energy you put out there is the energy you get to draw from. It's the mental practice of doing whatever it takes, whenever it's needed, to be totally present; using 100% of the energy you are granted every day productively and putting the best you forward. When the needed attitude isn't there, you actively pull from within what will *appear* to others as the needed attitude. Attitude precedes behavior. Whether this means turning up the charm instead of walking past someone, smiling when you feel like frowning, adjusting your attitude from "woe is me" to "I'm blessed," or moving from the natural desire to criticize to one of finding praise – just do it! Martin Buber called this, "the turning or being toward the other." That is, being fully present. The triggered responses in those around you will be favorable ones as opposed to negative ones. Despite not always wanting to play, once you learn how to Zing! it becomes second nature and you are able to do that which needs to be done. Success leads to success.

Thomas Huxley said, "Perhaps the most valuable result of all education is the ability to make yourself do the thing you have to do when it ought to be done, whether you like it or not; it is the first lesson that ought to learned; and however early a man's training begins, this is probably the last lesson he learns thoroughly." Are you able to do what needs to be done (when it needs to be done) whether you want to do it or not? Do you make the connection between your desire to lead and the potential outcome of your efforts?

Consider the potentially disastrous consequences of a surgeon who had an argument with her husband before going into surgery and can't let it go... would you like to be her patient? Imagine rearranging your work schedule to hear a motivational speaker who flew from one coast to another to give his speech but was resentful because he had to miss his kid's softball game and couldn't let it go...would you be all that inspired? And, think about the likely outcome of an encounter between two strangers when one of them doesn't feel worthy of "being met"... but, you enthusiastically prepared for your blind date, dressed in your favorite outfit and showed up with great optimism? The surgeon, speaker and single all had a decision to make: To Zing! (the verb) or risk the less desirable results. When you practice the skill of doing what it takes to get the job done (whether you want to or not) you'll recognize how quickly the rest of you joins in and before you know it, you are at your natural best. Life is easy again.

Principle Two: *There will always be obstacles, challenges and mountains to climb when you desire to lead your organization,* *seek to improve a social condition, right a wrong, improve your management team, parent responsibly, initiate change or serve a greater social good.*

The problems in this world are fixable and the everyday challenges you face manageable. You have what it takes to make a difference and better influence the outcome of your efforts. Incorporating the many Insights of Zing! into your daily routine will require considerable effort and the acceptance of the emotional, physical, spiritual and psychological energy need to make change happen. Not everyone has what it takes to walk the talk. Despite being good at the talk, some individuals fall short on the execution as soon as they realize Zing! is work. Most things worth achieving will require overcoming some form(s) of opposition or competing force.

If Leadership Were Easy

If leadership was easy, a nation's civil liberties wouldn't be at risk as we enter the 21st Century.

If leadership was easy, there would be all the resources needed to find a cure for Alzheimer's.

If leadership was easy, countries wouldn't be at war.

If leadership was easy, anyone who wanted a college education would be able to afford one.

If leadership was easy, those made homeless because of Katrina and other natural disasters would be home again - after almost four years!

If leadership was easy, the old man down the street wouldn't be splitting his daily medicine doses in half to make them last longer, his medical coverage would accommodate his medical needs - and the family next door without any health insurance, would have coverage.

If leadership was easy, children wouldn't go to bed hungry every night.

If leadership was easy, school teachers would be offered the salaries afford professional athletes.

If leadership was easy, drug dealers wouldn't be given better legal representation than the victims of their crime.

If leadership was easy, states would find a way to better care for their mentally ill.

If leadership was easy, qualified civic leaders could run for political office based upon their character, not their bank account.

If leadership was easy, everyone would be a leader.

How hard are you willing to work?

From running for class president, organizing a protest, spending spring break working for Habitat for Humanity to taking in a foster child, teaching someone to read, and becoming an advocate for children in the court system (via the CASA program), the intensity of your involvement and effort answers the question: How hard are you willing to work?

Principle Three: *The process of your leadership is one of positive, constructive, forward moving change; void of manipulation, corruption, deceit, power brokering and unethical behavior.*

Inherent within the philosophy of Zing! is a sense of fair play, critical thinking, well informed decision making, and the desire to protect other's basic human rights, as well as, your own. Zing! involves a continual internal dialogue about *how* to play the game using constructive, productive and civil "rules of engagement." Unfortunately, you can often reach great heights by using those around you as stepping stones. Just stack up those you have used, abused and manipulated and you have made a staircase to your next promotion or goal. In truth, you have cheated your integrity and negatively impacted your ability to positively influence those around you. It matters *how* you achieve. It matters *how* you influence others. It matters that it matters. Be concerned about the "rules of engagement" or the process you use to influence others; choose to be positive in your approach.

Rules of Engagement:

- Being respectful of those you serve;
- Being courteous;
- Avoiding "kissing up" for the sake of personal advantage;
- Being civil in your actions and language (i.e. not yelling, not swearing or being degrading);
- Giving credit where credit is due;
- Not over exaggerating your qualifications or expertise;
- Striving do your best;
- Owning your failures without blaming others;
- Approaching situations as part of the solution;
- Honoring your commitments; and
- Operating out of wisdom – not ignorance (i.e. being well informed).

Principle Four: *The outcome of your efforts is nothing less than a better you and a better world; a decision to have Zing! is a commitment to serving the greater social good one person at a time.*

Hitler was a phenomenal leader by most traditional models of leadership. He falls short when held to the standards of Zing! because of the horrific and self-serving outcomes of his leadership. Leaders who rise to the heads of their corporations, only to build their own fortunes at the expense of their employees and share holders aren't leaders; they are "criminals" who are rarely punished for their disservice to humanity because they have outsmarted, out paid and manipulated the system in their favor. Leading and living with Zing! is not a game of Simon Says where only one person is left standing; either everyone wins in the end, or no one wins.

Serving a greater social good is the realization we are all in this thing called life together. We share one planet. We are but one humanity. There doesn't have to be winners and losers, those that are in and those that are out, or the privileged and the underprivileged. Serving a greater social good involves the realization of how your daily efforts impact something greater than you and your immediate surroundings. This sentiment is found in the following writing by Pastor Martin Neimoller:

Someone to Stand Up
In Germany, they first came for the Communists and
I didn't speak up because I wasn't a Communist.

Then they came for the Jews and I didn't speak
up because I wasn't a Jew.

Then they came for the trade unionists and

I didn't speak up because I wasn't a trade unionist.

Then they came for the Catholics and I didn't speak up because I was a Protestant.

Then they came for me - and by that time, no one was left to speak up.

Examples of Serving a Greater Social Good:

- Standing up for those segments of the population which remain underrepresented and forgotten;
- Working to re-write your company's policies perpetuating prejudice;
- Advocating for individual freedoms and the sustaining of civil liberties;
- Improving a social condition;
- Raising children (or your neighbor's children) with positive self-esteem;
- Caring and advocating for safe and fair labor practices;
- Protecting children;
- Offering quality education to all of the world's citizens;
- Speaking up for those without a voice (like victims of sexual assaults); and
- Changing things for the better of all of humankind.

Although these goals may appear overly optimistic or not "your job," consider personalizing the list above by reflecting upon ways you can positively impact your immediate environment, residence hall, organization, youth group, hometown, place of work, neighborhood and community. What involvements, people, projects or conditions in your eye sight could be improved if you focused on them?

Exploration: Moment of Truth

Directions: Use the space below to list as many target areas for your talents (Zing!) in your immediate environment. What and who could and should benefit from your potential to positively change the situation or outcome?

_____

_____

_____

_____

_____

_____

_____

_____

Beliefs of Zing!

The four underlying Principles of Zing! are supported through the 21 Insights and accompanying modifications to your attitudes and behaviors. Your personality develops throughout the process of having Zing! and you will realize what you thought to be true about life and leadership isn't true at all. The following beliefs are examples of conclusions drawn by individuals who have experienced significant maturation, growth and personal development.

Zing! Belief: *You do get a second chance to make a good first impression.*

This statement acknowledges the fact you are human. You will screw up. You will walk out of a bathroom with toilet paper stuck to the bottom of your shoe. Buttons will pop. Zippers will unzip. Because you are tired, words you've just invented will spill out of your mouth, you'll say things you don't mean, and neglect to say things you should. More often than not, you have time to fix what you momentarily break, apologize, or make it right. I caution you against writing someone or something off prematurely (including you).

Zing! Belief: *Sometimes, you've just got to let it go!*
If the damage is too great to repair, remember this second principle and LET IT GO! It's over. You can't turn back the clock or erase a memory in someone else's mind. For example, think of your entire high school experience minus a day or two or your first day on a college campus. Remember walking into the wrong class and staying there for the entire duration of class because you didn't want anyone else to know you were a freshman? For those of us who have tripped going up stairs, we share the bond of knowing what it feels like to try to act like nothing ever happened, despite hearing, "Good thing you weren't going down the stairs – that could have been really dangerous!" (I wasn't amused either.) Not all of your blunders are as bad as you think. Don't get hung up on things you can't change or control; just let it go!

> *My Most Embarrassing Moment*
> *The flight was departing Washington, D.C. I look forward to flying out of D.C. because I usually meet interesting people. For this reason (and to make myself feel better) I try to look respectable. This flight was no exception. During the boarding process I decided to use the closest restroom in the front of the plane.*

> *I learned a valuable lesson on this flight: You must never forget to securely lock the restroom door! There I was, minding my own business. As the door of the "occupied" restroom flew open, I quickly looked down to see very expensive Italian shoes. As if in slow motion, my eyes moved upward catching every thread, crease, monogram, and lapel pin. Eventually, my eyes made contact with those of a United States Senator.*

His face was a patriotic red as he quickly slammed the restroom door shut. I locked it and immediately went into panic mode.

I didn't move. Despite repeated requests from the flight attendant to return to my seat, I stayed put until the pilot finally "requested" I take my seat. Pulling myself together, I left the security of the restroom. What were the odds that the Senator and I were seated together anyways? I naively thought on my way back to my seat.

Oh, yes! My travel companion and I had met earlier. He sat reading his Wall Street Journal (upside down) and I quietly said, "Excuse me," as I took my seat. He never looked up. He never said a word. What exactly did I expect him to say, "Nice to see you again"? I picked up my book and started reading. It was over. I let it go.

Zing! Belief: *I'm OK, you're OK.*

I've already established that I'm short. This doesn't mean I always wanted to be short. In fact, I've always wanted to be ten inches taller. I'd look thinner and could find my way out an exit door in a crowded theatre without having to hold onto my husband's shirt. But in reality, I am vertically challenged at five feet plus a quarter-inch. This is the way it is. Improving your ZQ is not a sign of weakness or criticism. It is evidence of your desire to be better, smarter, and happier. Have enough self-esteem to welcome evaluation, criticism, and praise.

Zing! Belief: *Don't expect different results by repeating the same behaviors.*

As simple as this may sound, it's worth pointing out the obvious. In order to enhance, improve, increase, and change your current charismatic potential, you need to start behaving and thinking differently. You can't say you want to go from being a C student to an A student using the same study habits that got you all those C grades in the first place. You can't say (and I've tried) you are "officially dieting" and sit on the couch watching ESPN workout programs while eating a bag of potato chips. Change requires you *do something* differently than you are currently doing; whether by adding, revising, or deleting, it is now your job to leave your comfort zone and experiment. Nothing changes if nothing changes.

Zing! Belief: *Moving forward is easier with built in support systems.*

Change of any kind is easier when you have a supportive network or some form of accountability. If you are motivated by the freedom that comes with the decision to add Zing! to your life than you might not need additional structures to keep you on task and working towards specific behavioral and attitudinal changes. Whether trying to stay in shape or meet writing deadlines, for example, I have found it helpful to include a variety of motivational techniques in my plan. These range from prayer to the joy of being in my new office surrounded by pictures of my family, bright colors, and spectacular views. Support systems are personal. For someone other than you to identify what you need to keep moving towards Zing! is comparable to asking a travel agent to get you the cheapest flight possible to Bermuda without telling him what airport you will be departing from! We all need different things based upon our individual situations.

Ways to Achieve Sources of Support:

- Enlist the support of a friend to read this book with you.
- Get a calendar or journal to record one step you are taking every day – for thirty days – to become more charismatic.

- Identify someone to serve as your "coach" who can follow your progress and keep you to task. If they are a professional coach, they can also provide additional assessment techniques and strategies for enhanced influence.
- Set small, obtainable goals (i.e. to work on one Insight a week) and reward yourself upon accomplishment of each goal.
- Surround yourself with inspirational visual reminders or posters of Zing! people you admire.
- Continue to read books or studies on influence, leadership and charisma building.
- Attend leadership seminars and any personal development training available.
- Visit www.igot2know.com for on-line positive life lessons.

Chapter 8

FINDING ZING!

"Nothing ever great was achieved without enthusiasm."
- Ralph Waldo Emerson

The *Zing! Impact Equation* was first developed in 2004 to explain how leadership happens; the dynamic and ever changing set of circumstances interfacing to affect your potential to "override competing forces to positively influence others towards a greater social good." Since then, it has proven to be an effective non-threatening way to illustrate the interaction and complexity among active ever changing variables while providing a visual explanation of the significance of each variable in the equation – especially your role.

Originating from Moos' Environmental Theory (1980), the Zing! Impact Equation recognizes the impact of where you are when you are called to live a happier life, build better relationships (or get one), become a better parent, leader and/ or positively influence others. Moos' work is at the core of significant subsequent attempts to predict behavior including the popular personality style inventories or color theories. Moos noted that behavior (B) is a function (f) of the person (P) plus their environment (E) as presented in the equation: $B = f(P) + E$. When you change any part of the equation and you change the potential outcome: someone who comes off shy in public, can be far from shy in private; certain children end up learning considerably more once they change teachers; and athletes are known to perform at higher levels when playing in front of a crowd. The environment changed resulting in significant changes of behavior.

If the environment remains constant and you change the person variable, you also get a different outcome. What happens to attendance on the following Sunday the beloved pastor informs their congregation they will have a "guest" preacher next week? I can assure you, it either goes way up, or way down. It doesn't remain the same. Think back to your own behavior when you learned you would have a "substitute" teacher! How much learning (behavior) actually occurred on those days?

The overall behavior (B) outcome of Moos' Environmental Theory is called the *Zing! Quotient* (ZQ), the person (P) refers to the individual seeking to influence (that's you) in both equations, and the environment (E) is expanded in the Zing! Impact Equation to suggest a unique awareness to the reality: You always have an opportunity to influence others; whether in an elevator, behind a podium, walking your dog, communicating via email, or in someone's head. You aren't just part of an "environment," you are intentionally aware that your presence is significant to that time and place. This variable is called, *Environment of Opportunity*. The remaining two elements (*21 Insights* and *Individual Detractors*) represent attributes you should adopt or delete as identified by leading experts in life and leadership. The diagram below illustrates how it all comes together. Each part of the equation is explained in more detail in the paragraphs to follow.

Zing! Impact Equation

Zing! Quotient = f(Person) + Environment of Opportunity + 21 Insights − Individual Detractors

Abbreviated Zing! Impact Equation

$$ZQ = f(P) + EO + 21I - ID$$

Zing! Quotient (ZQ). When you consistently achieve what you set out to achieve your ZQ continues to grow. Other's faith in you also grows. Doors begin to open. You will find yourself in more and more situations where others willingly get behind your vision because you have what they would describe as a "positive track record," or "what it takes" to get the job done. Building a high ZQ coincides with the development of your positive reputation as a leader and the effectiveness your life is having on others.

The Zing! Impact Equation is only an equation or a guide designed to make sense of something complicated. The real test of your Zing! is in the results. You will know your ZQ is going up when things (including people) begin to change as a result of your influence. Maybe it's not what you had hoped to accomplish, but you will know you have Zing! when positive things begin to happen because of your life. Perhaps better systems have been put into place, awareness to your cause has increased, a child is smiling more often or you've learned how to listen for understanding. This is one reason why you don't need to be in a position of leadership to lead − a title isn't a result. You (the person) is where Zing! begins.

Person (P). You are the person (P) in the equation. Everything you bring with you wherever you go − from your personality to your appearance. Consider the complexity of responses when someone asks, "Tell me about yourself?" Do you tell them your likes and dislikes? Do you give a condensed version of your credentials? Do you speak of where you've been and where you want to go? Do you describe your height and weight? You can put forth the best you if you chose to do so, and need to in order to increase your ZQ.

Many things, like those listed below, combine to define you and are under your control. They represent the sum total of who you've chosen to become. Unlike the more traditional belief that someone with "charisma" looks a certain way, or has exceptional public speaking skills, the Zing! Impact Equation breaks down numerous aspects of your personality and presence so you have more to work with! You also have more to work on! As you take an initial look at the list, pick two people you know (one from a more formal setting and one from an informal setting) and consider what they would say about your (fill in the item.) If you have no idea, that's OK. That's why you are reading this book.

Attributes of the Person (You)

Intelligence
Disposition
Communication Skills
Sense of Humor
Outlook on Life
Use of Language
Appearance
Sense of Self
Compassion
Brain Dominance
Risk taking

Comfort
Social Circle/ Associations
Style
Faith
Confidence
Reputation
Physical Conditioning
Aspirations
Temperament
Sensitivity

The person (P) part of the equation is a summation of all the things that others sense, feel, assume or know about you, including your personality. That's why when you have Zing! you learn to use "what you've got" in the right setting and ask, "What do I need to turn up or communicate about myself at this moment to be more effective?" Perhaps smiling, taking a few steps towards someone and putting out your hand to start a conversation with a stranger is appropriate. At other times, letting someone else have the last word and listening more attentively will serve you better. [One of the best ways to continuously enhance your knowledge of the attributes others see is to start actively observing others. Study body language, expressiveness in conversation and spatial proximity. Observe what topics are brought up, the frequency and content of jokes told, and choice of attire. Become a creature of curiosity and start noticing (even recording) what appears to be effective engagement techniques. When possible, observe public speakers and professors to study how they make their points. Somewhere along the way they have learned how to master the Art of Being Present. Unlike the majority of people who don't make a living as the result of how they communicate, these two groups of individuals offer great lessons on being persuasive, personable, likeable, articulate and influential. Watch them if you can!]

Environment of Opportunity (EO). Wherever you go… there you are and people are watching. Your Environment of Opportunity (EO) represents all the means you have to influence others. Whether formal or informal, you have numerous venues and methods at your disposal for overriding competing forces to positively influence others. The extent to which you are also able to recognize unique opportunities to influence will play a major role in your Zing! potential. For example, are you willing to put yourself at the helm of an organization, run for a political office or join in a protest rally? Are you willing to pick up the phone, send an email or write a letter to someone you've just met and find interesting?

Any way you can make yourself "present" constitutes your Environment of Opportunity. You don't always need to be physically present to be present to others. Someone who thinks about you, maybe even makes the comment, "I wish (your name) could see this!" is illustrating the significance of presence. In addition, coaching a little league team, helping someone cross the street, hugging a crying child, complimenting your secretary, or sending flowers to someone are all ways to be present in someone else's environment. When a child says, "I shouldn't do this; my coach wouldn't like it" illustrates how the presence of the relationship influences the child's decision-making.

Another kind of presence or environment is the "human aggregate." This environment is created when a collection of individuals come together. The environment of a room filled with college students, for instance, is different when that same room is filled with sixth-graders. "Mandatory" audiences, for example, create a different learning environment than those who come of their own free will. The environment of a room filled with your relatives, for example, is different from a room filled with strangers. Expand your awareness of your environment to include the samples below, and you will expand your ZQ.

Environments of Opportunity:

- community and civic involvements
- positions of leadership
- means of communication
- other's expectations of you
- actual physical location
- thoughts others have of you
- home life
- external weather conditions
- place of employment or study

Too often, your ZQ is lowered because you don't take advantage of ways to reach out and share your vision, life or leadership. You forget to be creative in determining the scope of your Environment of Opportunity or hold back out of fear over possibly embarrassing yourself or actually making a worthwhile connection which might "raise the bar" on other's expectations of you. Your ZQ is lowered when you forget to send a "thank you" card, flowers or call someone who has assisted you in your mission – or, make the mistake of "shooting off an email" when a personal contact was needed. Awareness to the diversity of environmental opportunities to influence will keep your ZQ going in the right direction – up!

21 Insights. Of great value to the Zing! Impact Equation is the contribution made by each of the 21 Insights (21I) of Zing! which were identified after considerable investigation into the work of the more popular tried and true leadership/organizational authors and most admirable contributors to the greater social good. These sources are found in the Bibliography. Drawing from their inspirational strategies, laws, principles, lessons, habits and even a few "fish" tales, various insights (21 to be exact) emerged that were consistent across many resources and frequently supported by research. Additional criteria included two decades of my own observations motivating and developing leaders, very real lessons learned through personal life experiences and knowledge gained from informal conversations.

I recently asked a professional recruiter about the most sought-after characteristics of her top candidates. She commented, "A host of things – not just one. It's never just one thing." She observes candidates from the time they arrive to the interview to how they treat the wait-staff during lunch. She also spoke about the importance of integrity and how she evaluates this trait in a very short time with a candidate. Her observations of the smaller things lead her to big conclusions and important decisions.

When you buy into a majority of the Insights offered on the following pages for the majority of the time, you will achieve greater results than if you only adopt a few once in a while. In this case, more is better! You can go from wanting to achieving; from observing to doing. Your goal is to maximize your effort to learn about all 21 Insights not just the ones that come easy to you. Eventually, you will use the right skill or attitude at just the right time. This ability differentiates those who "get it" from those who don't know where to find it.

Attributes Found in the 21 Insights:

- The ability to self-examine
- A congruent content of character
- A clearly defined purpose
- A clearly articulated vision for the future
- Courage
- The ability to transcend adversity
- Adaptability
- A positive attitude
- The habit of praising others
- The ability to show respect
- The ability to nourish your mind, heart and soul
- Intelligence (or love of learning)
- Determination
- The ability to actively listen
- Interpersonal communication skills
- The pursuit of public speaking opportunities
- The ability to maintain and create healthy relationships
- A fun sense of humor
- Playfulness
- Self-discipline
- Humility

The more you use the Insights, the higher your ZQ; practice will make perfect if you practice correctly! At first, you may have to consciously think about employing a particular Insight because they won't always come naturally – even to the most effective of relationship builders and communicators! For example, Insight Fourteen is the Art of Interpersonal Communication. You can study this Insight, major in communication studies in college, attend numerous workshops on enhancing your communication skills, and still screw it up! Have you ever finished someone else's sentence for them not because you wanted to have them feel what you had to say was more important than what they had to say, but rather because you were so excited about their dialogue you couldn't help yourself? You had the best of intentions, but poor execution. Unfortunately, despite my sincere desire to make everyone feel valued in my presence, I admit to a poor memory when it comes to names. Having to casually look at someone's name tag to recall their name, or worse yet, appear as if I don't remember it (which is the sad truth) making them feel as if I didn't value the last time we were together. My heart is in the right place but my memory isn't in my head... it's elsewhere.

Individual Detractors (ID). The final part of the Zing! Impact Equation is identified by those things you do and fail to do which literally subtract from your potential effectiveness and influence. Perceived as negatives, Individual Detractors (ID) represent distractions to your message, inconsistencies between your talk and your walk and inappropriate behaviors (like forgetting someone's name you've known for years.) When you can reduce or completely eliminate these subtractions you will have a higher ZQ.

As an observer of human behavior, I'm amazed at how much attention people give to the "big stuff" and how they don't do the "easy stuff." Based upon the Zing! theory both kinds of "stuff" have the same potential to either raise or lower your ZQ. You can have all 21 Insights down, be at the right place and at the right time, and nail your presentation; but if you yawn without covering your mouth – which projects apparent boredom with everything and everyone around you – and that small, yet significant, action is noticed by all, the latter has far outweighed the former. You blew it. Why would you spend hours preparing a presentation, rehearse for hours, and then forget to cover your mouth when you yawn in public? Are you suggesting that the people around you need to be excited in your presence, but you don't need to be excited in their presence? Knowing instinctively which skill set or behaviors not to employ at any given time can be as valuable as knowing all 21 Insights.

Although Individual Detractors are as different as people, there are many commonly agreed upon negatives or subtractions to your personal magnetism which need to be eliminated. These detractors can be things you don't say or don't do, as well as, those you say and do. After you review the following sample of "Zing! zappers" go back through the list and place a check mark next to those you tend to do out of habit. Also remember offensive language, insults, off color remarks and poor taste is in the eye of the beholder. Not everything on the list below is going to qualify as a negative to you, maybe you find these items acceptable – even as positives. You wouldn't be reading this book if you didn't have a need to become more aware of your current influence or what might be holding you back from enhanced happiness, satisfaction and living a more meaningful life. Therefore, the items below aren't negotiable and the list isn't inclusive of all those small things that have big negative consequences.

Examples of Individual Detractors:

Over-exaggerating your accomplishments
Finding faults not remedies
Being ignorant of current affairs
Telling racist or sexist jokes
Talking credit for work you didn't do
Arriving late or leaving early
Being inconsiderate of other's feelings
Monopolizing a conversation
Using others for personal gain
Acting rude behavior or lacking manners
Having poor or no table etiquette
Appearing disorganized
Misrepresenting the truth
Gossiping
Not returning phone calls promptly
Being negative and pessimistic
Having personal hygiene "gross outs"
Taking things that aren't yours
Being disruptive when others are trying to listen
Acting out of ego
Forgetting people's names
Not smiling when passing someone
Failing to maintain eye contact
Taking your shoes off in others' presence
Clicking the end of pen in a distracting manner
Cutting ahead of others on line
Bragging about not reading
Monopolizing conversations
Appearing to be disorganized
Staying too long (or not long enough) at social functions

Looking at his or her watch during a conversation
Smoking without asking if others mind
Caring little about others' welfare
Boasting about being "bored"
Bragging about being "dumb"
Speaking with food in his or her mouth
Raising your voice or yelling at others
Failing to keep confidences

What's missing from the list above? Can you identify specific behaviors or attributes in people you know who just seem to fall short on the charismatic scale? Strive to maximize your ZQ and you find more Zing! in your life. The next chapters will review the 21 Insights in more detail, continue to offer opportunities for self-exploration and inspire you to seek that which you deserve – happiness!

Exploration: Eye of the Beholder Negatives

Directions: Take a moment to add to the list above by thinking of specific negatives that in your eyes make someone have less Zing! than if they eliminated them.

_____

_____

_____

_____

_____

_____

How Low Can We Go Club

Just when I think I've seen it all, I get on yet another plane! On a flight into Washington, D.C., a well-dressed man took his seat in the first class cabin. I sat directly behind him. Using

my exceptional detective skills, I pegged him as a regional vice-president for some company because that's what it said on his luggage tag.

Shortly before takeoff, I noticed this hadn't been a good day for him. I also noticed he was going to make sure it wasn't a good day for anyone else. Maybe it was the manner in which he literally chucked a bag of pretzels back at the flight attendant because "he expected more out of First Class" or the fact he took off his shoes, leaving his stinky feet for the rest of us to smell, which demonstrated his self-serving approach to life. He might have looked like a million bucks, but I wouldn't give two cents for his opinion about anything.

At least he was in good company. Although I wasn't invited to join "the club," it appeared some were in the midst of an active recruitment campaign for the How Low Can We Go Club. For instance, the woman seated behind me discussed her divorce loudly on her cell phone. For the rest of us (including the pretzel-chucking, foot-smelling VP), this meant acting as if we couldn't hear what should have been a very personal and private conversation. When the woman sitting to her left (apparently not invited to join the club either) commented that it sounded like she was going through a tough time, my write - in candidate for president's ZQ plummeted with a sharp, "Why don't you mind your own business?!" That would have been a nice option.

Cell Phones: The Great Detractors

Poor cell phone etiquette is one of the more prevalent Individual Detractors of our time. From continuing your conversation while trying to order a coffee at Starbucks to filling the romantic sounds of a dim lit restaurant with your one way cell phone conversation, there are times when you shouldn't be talking on your cell phone, or taking calls! And not because you want privacy; but rather because other people shouldn't have to hear your conversation! While on the subject, I consistently hear of professional people who meet for lunch and one spends the entire time taking calls and checking his/her palm pilot. This behavior sends a clear message to the other person trying to actually have a lunch meeting with you they aren't worthy. The same negative impressions are achieved when you call someone and proceed to constantly take other incoming calls, putting them on "hold." What messages are you communicating with the way you use your cell phone or portable technology?

Zing! Momentum: Proceed with Caution

As you review the many insights offered on the following pages, your friends, family, colleagues, associates, and neighbors, for instance, will almost immediately interact with you differently; and you will respond to them differently. As this momentum builds, you will experience a satisfying sense of accomplishment. A word of caution, however: others may not always appreciate your efforts for self-improvement, especially if they are accustomed to interacting with the more self-focused you. They may become confused or question your motives. The best way to proceed is to be consistent.

Characteristics of influence need to be applied consistently across all aspects of your life. Being an effective mediator at work, for example, should imply you are also an effective mediator at home. If I observe you yelling at your child in the grocery store, then I'm not likely to walk into your office for counsel because

I'm having trouble with a subordinate. Likewise, you can't expect me to confide in you as a friend after you've just shared extremely personal information about a mutual acquaintance. Nothing is more disturbing than meeting career counselors who hate their jobs, healthcare professionals who smoke or are grossly unfit, or receiving notes home from your child's teacher containing spelling errors. Consistency in your behaviors signals the commitment you have to personal growth.

Chapter 9

INSIGHT ONE
The Opportunity of Self-Inspection

*"Have you learned lessons only of those who
admired you, and were tender with you, and stood aside
for you? Have you not learned great lessons from those
who rejected you, and braced themselves against
you, or disputed passage with you?*
- Walt Whitman

When you put on a pair of overalls, you are ready to overhaul just about anything! Similarly, when your office gets a new document shredder, papers that were once significant are now disposable. When your neighbor gets a twenty-five cubic foot dumpster, you go to bed thinking of things to discretely toss in it! Whether a pair of overalls, document shredder, or large dumpster, opportunities will arrive in your life, daring you to evaluate what's important, useful, underused, insignificant, or overrated.

In the early 1990s, leadership experts and researchers Warren Bennis and Robert J. Thomas interviewed an assortment of leaders in search of common characteristics of leadership and found results essential to our discussion of influence almost twenty years later. Their research revealed the role of "reflective structures."[1] Specifically, successful leaders had a collection of similar traits, including time and space allocated for self-examination. For some individuals, this translated as daily exercise; for others, religious prayer. Some leaders took "sabbaticals;" others took numerous "mini-vacations." How you choose to remove yourself from distraction to allow for personal questioning and soul-searching doesn't matter. The important thing is that you get in the habit of spending time focusing inward.

Exploration: Self-Inspection Inquiry

Directions: Take a moment to consider when, where and how you will incorporate reflective structures into your day. Record ideas on the lines below and then pick one to start today!

_____

_____

_____

_____

_____

Self-inspection is a process of self-discovery. It's not about telling you what you want to hear, but about being truthful. Effective leaders and individuals with Zing! constantly seek ways of soliciting feedback about their performance, effectiveness, and areas of needed improvement. They are open to others' opinions of them and are not threatened or intimidated by evaluative measures. Likewise, they know and appreciate the many benefits of being receptive to suggestion or feedback. In return, they give and receive evaluation in an environment free from judgment, personal attacks, and incivility. Evaluation may be uncomfortable, but it doesn't have to be hurtful.

Have you ever been told "You're not living up to your potential?" Do you remember your reaction? Eleanor Roosevelt once said: "People can't make you feel inferior without your consent." Her statement suggests the power of interpretation and perspective. The ability to remove negative emotions from statements (or observations) about your performance is a skill. Instead of becoming defensive, for example, check your emotions. Apply the criticism to a specific behavior. You can change behaviors. Don't miss the benefits because you are too sensitive because self-examination is an important tool of growth. Refuting the evidence or blaming the evaluator (even if that's you) doesn't make the observation any less true. Self-examination is not free of criticism – or praise. It is important to examine what you do well, as well as how others receive your strengths and weaknesses. Exchange your need to be liked for the higher need of pursuing what really matters: Truth. The benefits of knowing where you excel or need to improve far outweigh the temporary discomforts or nagging, unsubstantiated suspicions held inside. Specifically, the very process of personal examination takes you to a higher place.

Benefits of Self-Inspection:

- Achieving a more accurate perception of what others find appealing and not appealing;
- Improving your potential to have better interpersonal relationships;
- Allowing you to be less defensive and more sensitive to others' needs;
- Enhancing your confrontation skills (the true love skill);
- Strengthening your self-confidence;
- Role-modeling strong character and desire for self-improvement;
- Making you more approachable (especially by subordinates);
- Making you a better student of life and leadership;

- Enhancing your skills of assessment;
- Allowing you to capitalize on your strengths and minimize your weaknesses;
- Helping you to re-direct your energies toward areas of greater need;

Because effective leaders continually strive to raise their personal bar of excellence, they also achieve higher levels of excellence. Self-inspection puts you in a continual state of growth and development. This can keep you alive and moving forward. To do nothing as the world changes around you is to actually lose ground; you are no longer "in style." You risk not living up to your potential the day you believe you have already maximized it! As you work through the Insights in the following chapters, remain open to the process and accept you are being human if you experience insecurity, fear, internal chaos, rejection, vulnerability, lowered confidence, or unexpected internal resistance. Self-inspection will require you to do something with the information, has the potential to open old wounds and requires new skills. This is the price to pay for getting what you want.

Many of the Insights to follow have accompanying exercises, some of which are found directly in the chapter text, while others are longer and have been placed in their own Appendix. You can choose to take them now, write directly in this book or take them when you are in the right frame of mind and have more time – but do them!

Exploration: The Truth on Moving Forward

Directions: How do you feel about looking inward so you can move onward? Take a minute to consider whether the following statements are true or false by placing a T or F next to each statement.

_____ I am confident in my abilities.

_____ I am not open to feedback about my skills.

_____ I effectively give feedback to others regarding their skills.

_____ I rarely take time to examine my own weaknesses.

_____ I actively seek self-improvement opportunities.

_____ When criticized, I blame someone or something else.

_____ I have created space in my life for self-reflection.

_____ I am afraid of what self-examination will tell me.

_____ I find growth potential in hearing others' opinions of my skills.

_____ I am perfect – just the way I am.

Confidentiality Speaking

Have you ever met anyone who shared his or her entire life history in the first five minutes of conversation? You walked away thinking: That was more information than I needed to know! When you build "reflective structures" into your daily life and leadership, you will collect information *from* you and *for* you. Honor your right to privacy. Respect others' rights to their privacy. Just because someone asks you about personal matters doesn't mean you have to share the results of your latest self-assessment! I recommend you keep the results to yourself unless you are sharing the information for developmental purposes with a supportive party.

Influence 1 Initiatives

- Spend fifteen minutes a day observing others' behaviors. Write down what you found appealing and/or not appealing. Compare these behaviors to your own.

- For 14 consecutive days, schedule an activity of self-reflection in which you give yourself time and space to contemplate your ability to handle what that day brings. This could be a bike ride, walk around the block, writing in a journal, meditation, and so on.

- Go to your bookstore and pick up three self-help books that focus on those parts of your life that you need to improve. Read them.

- Listen quietly the next time someone tries to tell you something about your attitude or behavior.

- Refrain from making any response other than to re-iterate what you hear them trying to tell you.

- Focus on potential "signs" providing feedback about your Zing! Quotient. For example, are you left out of certain discussions? Do people avoid making eye contact with you?

- Be willing to risk hearing the truth.

- Solicit comments about your personality from friends, co-workers, and even complete strangers.

- Consider hiring a coach or counselor to assist you in translating or processing your self-discoveries.

Chapter 10

INSIGHT TWO
The Content of Character

*"There are those who believe something, and therefore
tolerate nothing; and on the other hand, those who
tolerate everything, because they believe nothing."*
- Robert Browning

One of the most inspirational places to stand in all of America is at the foot of the Lincoln Memorial in Washington, D. C. Standing in front of Abraham Lincoln you are inspired to never tell another lie – regardless of how small. I'm not sure why, but something abo ut his enormous, concrete presence inspires truthfulness. Perhaps his magnetic pull originates with the image of "Honest Abe" taught to us when we were young. Unfortunately, we grow up and forget this internal source of self-respect: Truthfulness.

Leadership authority and motivational speaker, Brian Tracy, identified in his bestselling book *Create Your Own Future*, the twelve critical factors of unlimited success. Like other leadership resources, he included the role of character. Tracy contends, "The universal truth is that you inevitably attract into your life the people, circumstances, ideas, opportunities, and resources that are in harmony with your dominant thoughts. You can never achieve on the outside what you have not earned on the inside."

Content of character is the essence of who you are when all of your possessions are gone. It consists of the values and virtues you possess and how they direct your behaviors, treatment of others and the legacy you will leave. A quick way to discover your content of character is to stand in a room by yourself and ask, "Do I like the company I'm keeping?" While there, you can also ask the following questions of character:

Do I take unfair advantage of others?
Am I just in my reasoning?
Am I capable of deceiving those who trust in me?
Does personal gain make my moral decision making conditional?
Would I behave differently if I knew I wouldn't get caught?
Am I proud of my treatment of (fill in the name)?
Do I know what I stand for these days?
How do I define honesty?

If you were a tree, character would represent your root system. It is what makes you strong or weak, truthful or deceitful and a hard worker or a "slacker." Character is transparent. When held up to other virtues, it holds its own. How others perceive your character is a significant determining factor in whether or not they will be influenced by you. Competency without character, for instance, may look good on the outside, but on the inside there isn't the substance to serve others.

Components of Character

Honesty. You are either an honest person or you are not an honest person. You can't be true to your content of character if you lie only once in a while, plagiarize only once per term paper, or take only a few things from the office. Dishonesty is dishonesty.

Cheating is cheating. Stealing is stealing. How much or how often is irrelevant. You either live your life according to a set of moral standards or you don't. Abraham Lincoln once said, "If I cannot trust you with the small things, don't expect me to trust you with the big things."

Integrity. Your actions speak to your values and your values drive your actions. Applied integrity lives at the core of your content of character. Your ability to "walk the talk" is so readily apparent to others that its absence creates disconnect – or distance – between you and your ability to influence others. You can't have Zing! without integrity because the resulting confusion immediately causes distrust which in a follower's perspective is a deal breaker. What reverence requires is a consistent and predictable set of behaviors. Others will always know what you represent and how you will behave because you have chosen to be predictable! Conclusions are drawn when inconsistencies appear or what you say isn't what you do.

For instance, do you say, "I am a team player," and then proceed to undermine your boss? Do you say, "I want to make the world a better place," and then fail to actively volunteer in your local school, YMCA, and/or hospital? Do you say, "My children and family are the most important things in my life," and then fail to sit down at least once a week for a family dinner? The hypocrisy of such character has become the legacy left to our children, and frankly, to our society. Integrity is predictability of your actions. Demonstrate what you stand for by living it.

Trust. The interesting thing about this component of character is that it takes a long time to build and only seconds to destroy. To build trust is to do what you say you will do and when you say you will do it, and if you don't you admit it. When you do this twenty-four hours a day, people give you the benefit of the doubt when discrepancies between your actions and your words arise.

They assume there is another explanation or something out of the ordinary has occurred. In other words, they trust your intentions and your potential has not been compromised. However, if others can't even hold you to your word, they will suspect everything you say – and do! They will question your motives and examine your statements carefully. They will start looking for ways to verify your statements by bringing other people and sources into your conversations. Trust grows over time.

Exploration: Trust Breakers

Directions: As you read through the following list of trust breakers, write the names of someone who trusts you greatly (Person A), not so much (Person B) and not at all (Person C.) For each, place a check mark under the trust breaker that applies to your relationship with that particular person. When done, consider why the issue mattered to that person.

	A	B	C
Took something of theirs, said you returned it, but you didn't.			
Said you would hold something in confidence, and you told someone.			
Always say you'll be there at a certain time, and arrive late.			
Promise to do something with them, and you cancel.			
Blamed someone else for something you actually did that was wrong.			
Exaggerated your accomplishments to gain their favor and they found out.			

Moral Decision Making. Consider these definitions: An unethical decision is a decision with the pay-off up front. An ethical decision is a decision with the pay-off down the line. Your morals represent your internal sense of right and wrong. They direct or lay the foundation for your decision making and connect to your value system. To be a person of great morality is to be guided by a clearly defined understanding of fairness, compassion, love, goodness, righteousness and justice. Rarely – if ever, do I hear someone say, "I respect you for cheating on your wife," or "I'm in awe of your ability to lie!"

Your ZQ will go down every time you cheat, steal someone else's ideas without giving the proper credit, and unfairly take advantage of someone or something. Just because you can get away with it doesn't make it right. Sometimes, you do have to "pay your dues," or wait until you've earned what you want. A desire for instant gratification or wanting more than you deserve often leads people to be dishonest, cheat, or manipulate a situation to their advantage.

Resisting the quick fix or temptation to "do what everyone else is getting away with" doesn't make it consistent with your morals. It's hard, but necessary, to worry only about your moral compass and let others be judged for theirs.

Values. What you hold to be important in life represents your values. In order to have a conversation about your purpose in life, you also need to discuss what matters to you; what are your values? From global issues to continuing your education, you can have values related to your vocation, as well as, what you choose to do on vacation! People with Zing! respect other's rights to determine what matters most to them and is free from judgment. John W. Gardner said, "Ultimately we judge our leaders in a framework of values."

The important lesson around values is that you *have* them. How would you answer the following value centered questions:

What do I represent?
What do I want my contribution in the world to be?
How do I define a "productive day?"
What does it mean to be in a friendship?
At the end of the day, if I've failed at what (fill in) nothing else matters?
What role should my talents play in my vocation?
Why is happiness important?
Why (or why not) does it matter how my children rate my parenting?

Conscience. The voices you hear in your head or the internal dialogue between what you want to do and what is the right thing to do is called your conscience. Despite the desired temporary break from knowing how to conduct your life, your conscience never shuts off. Regrettably, it does shut down and instead of having that "internal dialogue" like the angle and devil debating on your shoulders, you find yourself void of backbone. You get into situations where you literally ask yourself, "What was I thinking?" Allow yourself to be internally confused, torn or conflicted. This is how you know your conscience is bothering you. Something you are doing, or thinking, is inconsistent at the core. When this happens, listen! It's also a good strategy to avoid making decisions when you are emotionally worn down or overly stressed out and you can't handle internal conflict. Wait until you have the energy required for the internal debate or you might do something you will regret later.

Responsibility. Learn right from wrong then live right. Creating a greater good is (and always has been) inspired by a civic sense of duty, call to our individual responsibility and collective conscience. Your life is meant to lead. Your leadership is meant to be lived. You have been given great opportunities and now, as previously noted, have great reasonability to give back. Getting in the habit of "owning" the future begins by "owning" your present. Taking responsibility represents the long lost art of fundamentally caring about others, quality, productivity, and showing appreciation. When you take on the ownership of something, you are also making a significant value statement. What should you be caring for or about which is an inconvenience? Who has shown you guidance at their own personal expense?

Remembering Dr. Martin Luther King, Jr.

When I was a little girl playing on my swing set, Dr. Martin Luther King, Jr. was following his call to conscience and sense of responsibility for the civil rights of blacks. On April 4, 1967 he did not stray from his moral sense of obligation to the Civil Rights Movement when he spoke out against the war in Vietnam; rather he reiterated his theme: "violence is violence." Despite all of the criticism he took for delivering a speech which wasn't specifically about the movement, in his eyes, he had a responsibility based upon his fight against violence. He felt an obligation and took the risk. The following is an excerpt from "Beyond Vietnam" delivered at the Riverside Church.[1]

Finally, as I try to explain for you and for myself the road that leads from Montgomery to this place, I would have offered all that was most valid if I simply said that I must be true to my conviction that I share with all men the calling to be a son of the living God. Beyond the calling of race or nation or creed is this vocation of sonship and brotherhood. Because I believe that the Father is deeply concerned, especially for His suffering and helpless and outcast children, I come tonight to speak for them. This I believe to be the privilege and the burden of all of us who deem ourselves bound by allegiances and loyalties which are broader and deeper than nationalism and which go beyond our nation's self-defined goals and positions. We are called to speak for the weak, for the voiceless for the victims of our nations, for those it calls "enemy," for no document from human hands can make these humans any less our brothers.

Associations. Accept the reality your content of character will also be revealed through the people and things you spend time around. There will be a connection or impact on your reputation because of the values attributed to your friends, colleagues, company, fraternity brothers and clients. You will be known for those in your company. Unfortunately, you may discover the harm being done to your Zing! too late. When it is revealed, the key is to act quickly and distance yourself from those who clearly have given others reasons to question their character or perceive them in a negative light. You might not have known then, but you know now!

This point is made all too clear by Barack Obama's need during his presidential campaign to quickly distance himself from his former pastor Reverand Wright because of "disgraceful and divisive" comments made by Wright which ran contrary to Obama's beliefs and campaign message. When confronted, Wright didn't back away from his opinions. Instead, he publicly reinforced his inflammatory remarks. As Obama's numbers quickly dropped in the polls directly following the news of their relationship, Obama had to choose: do nothing, defend the relationship or distance himself. Understanding the power of your associations, Obama quickly and publically put miles between himself and his former pastor.

Insight 2 Initiatives

- Read the landmark speeches of Dr. Martin Luther King, Jr. found in *A Call to Conscience*.

- Do what you say you will do and when you say you will do it.

- Tell the truth. (Especially on the small stuff.)

- If you tell a lie, admit your mistake.

- Don't cheat.

- Never say (or believe): "Everybody else does it, so it's OK."

- Remember: What goes around comes around.

- Pay your dues; hard work does pay off.

- Hold yourself to a higher ethical standard than those around you; doing so will give them someone to look up to.

- Give credit where credit is due.

- Never cover up for someone else's unethical decision making.

Chapter 11

INSIGHT THREE
The Power of Purpose

*"When a man does not know what harbor
he is making for, no wind is the right wind."*
- Seneca

My son Jake used to love to fish. Now he loves to sail. I used to love to fish, and still do. Until rather recently, we fished behind our sailboat going out of the harbor into Buzzard's Bay. But now that my son has become a "pure" sailor (along with his sister) and my husband doesn't appreciate fishing when we should be sailing, I only get to fish when there is no wind. There's always wind in Buzzard's Bay. The "Three Sailing Amigos" are thrilled to see flags blowing so hard they almost shred. I see there will be no fishing that day. I've accepted the only things true sailors appreciate are wind, speed and apparent wind speed. There should be no lines trailing the boat only to get caught in a lobster pot - or Heaven forbid - slow down the boat. If I do get to put out a fishing line, the only fish I'm going to catch is one who can swim nine knots and has lips of steel. I'm determined, however, to pursue my passion for fishing!

Secretly, I've also thought about jumping aboard one of the boats featured on *The Deadliest Catch* as they venture into Alaskan waters to catch King Crab. I bet I could drop a line off one of those boats! I must admit: I never had the desire to be a brain surgeon, airline pilot, firefighter, second grade substitute teacher, or secret agent. Not because I wasn't willing to work that hard, but rather because none of it was something I wanted to do – way too scary for my liking. Is it possible I was born to fish? The older I get the more clear I am as to my purpose. Yet for many people, the question of purpose is forever looming overhead, especially if you are still in school or starting a career. A wise student once shared with me the following insight: There are only two truly difficult days in your life - the day you are born and the day you finally figure out why!

What is your purpose? How should you be spending your time? What do you want for your life and leadership? All of these questions can be answered when you slow down long enough to look at "life" from different perspectives. One approach is to consider life as a "job" – you get up, get dressed, and go to work! Attendance is required, if you don't play you don't get paid, and at the end of the day there is a performance review. A definite perk is you are self-employed making you the "boss of you." This allows you to choose what difference you will make in this world and define your own success, identify what brings you happiness and discover your true purpose.

Purpose of life defines what you are trying to achieve – as well as how you achieve it. Deepak Chopra in *The Seven Spiritual Laws of Success* says, "Everyone has a purpose in life…a unique gift or special talent to give to others. And when we blend this unique talent with service to others, we experience the ecstasy and exultation of our own spirit, which is the ultimate goal of all goals." *Purpose* represents the will to work or intention towards something. Indira Gandhi said: "The purpose of life is to believe, to hope, and to strive." Within these words is a larger philosophy of faith, future, and growth.

Purpose is more visible than your philosophy of life, as described below. Others can literally "see" your purpose or intention, whereas they "deduce" your philosophy of life. Your purpose is defined by your vocation or how you spend your time, where you put your energies, and toward what end you communicate to others. For example, people observe you teaching, preaching, coaching, or building. They notice you work hard, commit to an organization or employer, and conduct yourself professionally.

Purpose guides your direction and movement. Individuals with Zing! are attractive to others because they are obviously moving towards something. It doesn't have to be a single "great" thing like running a twenty-six million-mile marathon or building a new company so you can sell it in three years and retire. In fact, purpose can be a lot of little things done sooner not later. Purpose is your present! You instantly have Zing! when you can get out of bed every day with the immediate desire to be a productive and contributing member of society that day. Not everyone has the luxury or resources to do a single "great" thing, but we all have the ability to do many small things with greatness. Your present *is* your purpose. When you focus on the here and now, tomorrow takes care of itself.

Exploration: Zing! in a Word

Directions: What do you want to matter to you today? Sometimes an entire life of questioning can be deduced to a few words. Reflect upon the list of words below start by circling the ten that represent what you want to drive your life and leadership. Then your list back to only 5 words! If you are feeling daring, select the ONE word that inspires you.

Achievement	Goals	Patriotism	Trust
Action	Gratitude	Peace	Truth
Beauty	Greatness	Perfection	Understanding
Bravery	Growth	Perseverance	Values
Career	Happiness	Philanthropy	Virtue
Change	Health	Planning	Wealth
Charity	Honesty	Politeness	Winning
Children	Hope	Power	Wisdom
Common Sense	Humility	Praise	Wit
Confidence	Humor	Pride	Work
Conscience	Ideals	Progress	Youth
Contentment	Imagination	Purpose	Zeal
Courage	Individuality	Quality	
Curiosity	Intelligence	Reason	
Dignity	Justice	Reputation	
Education	Kindness	Respect	
Enjoyment	Leadership	Responsibility	
Equality	Learning	Security	
Excellence	Life	Service	
Experience	Love	Simplicity	
Faith	Loyalty	Solitude	
Family	Marriage	Spiritual	
Forgiveness	Money	Strength	
Freedom	Morals	Success	
Friendship	Obligation	Talent	
Generosity	Passion	Thinking	
Giving	Patience	Tolerance	

Focus on best the most excellent human being you can be today. Be considerate, work hard, say "Hello!" to everyone you see, and do something nice for someone today. This "one day at a time" approach is consistent with the building of reverence and inspiring followship. When you are always distracted, moving too fast or totally preoccupied with what appears to be so much "more important" than who is standing in front of you, you risk turning away those you could serve. Do your behaviors literally suggest you are too busy to be a positive part of *their* day?

Deciding what level of personal performance and expectations you want to live by is living your purpose as your present. Think about what standards of excellence you want to guide your life and leadership by asking: What do I seek in the present? Do I seek to be more personally magnetic to others and a happy contributing member of society? Am I doing things today that are bringing me pleasure, spreading joy, or have I decided to be resentful, angry and miserable today? Am I planning on skipping class to do my laundry today or do I want to maximize my learning potential?

Exploration: Standard Setting

Directions: Use the space provided below to write down ten words describing the level of performance or standards by which you choose to go through your daily existence.

_____

_____

_____

_____

_____

_____

You now have an idea of the level of performance you seek, what about the affect or emotional outcomes of your presence? What do you want for the kind of reaction or affect you will leave in those you influence on a daily basis? The argument has already been made for positively influencing others which implies there will be good feelings resulting from the expenditure of your energies in the present. Keep in mind, however, when Zing! people override competing forces to accomplish their goals, the competing forces are often poor or resistant attitudes. Not everyone will walk away from your Zing! encounters feeling warm and fuzzy - maybe just the opposite. This doesn't mean you haven't achieved your purpose. For example, when parents don't succumb to the immediate gratification of their child's wish to buy something new because they need to work for it, the child might not feel happy, but the parent has left the child with valuable lessons and has accomplished his or her purpose; to be a good parent.

Exploration: Affect Setting

Directions: Use the space provided below to describe the way you want people to think and feel after interacting with you or being on the receiving end of your Zing! efforts. Consider what you might be trying to accomplish today... how will someone be different because of your presence?

_____

_____

_____

_____

_____

_____

Defining Your Life

Building upon how you want to leave people feeling, as well as, at what level of excellence you want to conduct your daily life, the next consideration is that of motive – or philosophy. It answers the basic question: Why were you born? It is the starting point for all the decisions you make in life. Your philosophy of life is found in the things you cherish, love, value and determine to matter.

Change your philosophy of life when it no longer fits. Part of Zing! is being content with process of continual personal discovery. Your philosophy of life can be altered dramatically through life events, revelations, or come in and out of focus over time.

Exploration: Philosophy of Life Statement

Directions: Using the space provided below write your life philosophy statement by completing each sentence. Before you begin, think about the values that are important to you and what inspires your life and leadership.

Life is… _____

_____

_____

_____

_____

_____

What is important to me is… (Insert value statements) _____

_____

_____

_____

_____

_____

Therefore, I choose to live my life by… (Insert action words)

_____

_____

_____

_____

_____

Achieving through Goal Setting

Hal Urban, author of *Life's Greatest Lessons*, says, "Living without goals is like going on a trip without a destination. If you don't know where you're going, you'll probably end up nowhere and any road will get you there." Goals are the result of a clearly defined purpose – or direction – in life. They can have a time frame (such as lowering your blood pressure in six months) or be open-ended (such as staying in shape.) Goals necessitate action. To achieve a greater good requires you to set obtainable goals and plan accordingly. To have this thing called Zing! will require you to get a plan, as well. The only way to achieve goals is to identify them on paper, develop a plan which includes deadlines and outcome measures, and start exerting the necessary energy.

Goals are accomplished through *objectives*; defined as a short-term and easily measured action or task making something larger happen. Examples of objectives are the items found on daily "to do" lists. They manage movement towards a goal. If you set a goal of enhanced staff synergy, for instance, you accomplish it by establishing a variety of objectives, from planning team-building exercises to enhancing lines of communication through conference calls, follow up emails and weekly meetings. One objective usually won't get the job done. The more elaborate your goal, the more objectives needed. Therefore, if you want something, you need to break your goal down into smaller parts or objectives.

If you find one approach ineffective, try a different approach. You can change objectives without changing your goals. When I was working full time with two infants, I forgot this rule of thumb. Instead of changing direction, I allowed myself to be continually frustrated. I repeatedly hit my head against the proverbial brick wall, watched the bump on my head grow bigger, yet continued to blame the wall instead of redirecting my energies. You too, have choices when you hit a wall. Alter your approach by changing your objectives.

Once you put your objectives in motion, you begin to impact and influence the world around you. There is a great sense of accomplishment when you place a check mark next to an accomplished objective. Be careful to set realistic objectives and time lines for you and those in your organization. Otherwise, having too many objectives that need to be done too quickly, results in lower morale and frustration, instead of inspiring participation and rewarding your positive influence! Be realistic and forward thinking at the same time.

INSIGHT 3 INITIATIVES

- Make a list of all the things that truly matter to you.

- Talk about your goals out loud.

- Tell strangers how you want to serve a greater social good. Be specific.

- Write a business plan for your life.

- Ask How? to achieve what you want to achieve, not if it will ever happen.

- Read about individuals who have accomplished great things.

- Write your own story in a journal focusing on how it happened.

- Visit and make a stronger commitment to your spiritual development.

- Commit yourself to a volunteer activity in your immediate environment or local community.

- Let go of things that don't matter so you have room for what counts.

- Set deadlines. Self-imposed deadlines can easily be overlooked, so employ or enlist another external source to enforce your deadline.

Chapter 12

**INSIGHT FOUR
The Inspiration of Vision**

*"The consideration that human happiness
and moral duty are inseparably connected will
always continue to prompt me to promote the former
by inculcating the practice of the latter."*
- George Washington

When my daughter was younger, she wanted to be President of the United States. After all, she was born on the Fourth of July and has been rather patriotic ever since. Fireworks seem like an appropriate way to celebrate her birth. Not as interested in the Presidency as she was in her earlier years, Kaitlin remains open to Secretary of State or another position involving foreign relations and holds firmly to the belief world leaders should talk instead of fight if they truly want peace. She has always loved history and writing, and has her sights set on attending Boston College. I believe this is due to the college's commitment to the service of mankind, as well as, its proximity to Fenway.

Although the 2008 election reinforced my daughter's interest in the political realm, it also gave validity to concerns about the challenges of being a woman seeking one of the most powerful positions in the Free World. The status and reverence of the American Presidency has also declined over the last eight years; due in large part to the lack of personal charisma and leadership of George W. Bush as evidenced by historically low approval ratings. The next President will have to overcome the subsequent consequences of distrust, distaste and worse, disinterest, caused by someone in a position of leadership who wasn't a leader.

The good news: You can learn from watching ineffective leaders just as you can from watching those who inspire your followship because of their character, intelligence and type of person you perceive them to be! You can learn from reading biographies and autobiographies of inspiring individuals. My daughter, for example, continues to read everything written by, or about, Eleanor Roosevelt – some of which she's read more than once. It is personally gratifying to see her take an interest in the lives of other powerful female forces in history. After reading her autographed copy of Madam Secretary by Madeline Albrecht, Kaitlin commented how she could see herself in some diplomatic role encouraging world peace. I believe this is her vision.

Vision is the ability to see what isn't there with mystic clarity and is routinely found in high achieving individuals, Nobel Peace Prize winners, entrepreneurs, and in those who serve a greater social good. Those with vision often leave legacies larger than life. They begin as the idealists, dreamers and optimists – until they make it happen! Disneyland, iPods, Tupperware, cell phones, disposable contact lenses, and computers – all a result of the true visionaries.

Walt Disney said, "If you can dream it, you can achieve it." All too often we tend to "play it safe" and not risk the ridicule or self-humiliation of being labeled a "dreamer." What's wrong with being a dreamer? Without individuals to see things before they created them, we wouldn't have bridges, electric cars, and remote controls! We wouldn't have penicillin. Michelangelo wouldn't have painted the Sistine Chapel. Ted Turner wouldn't have created CNN and Bill Gates wouldn't have developed an operating system that revolutionized personal computers; nor would they have combined forces to inoculate third world countries. The ability to have a vision and communicate it to others is a significant and distinguishing skill of influence.

Exploration: Making Vision a Reality

Directions: Are you a visionary thinker? The questions below are designed to explore various behavioral outcomes of visionary thinkers. Take a moment and see if they apply to you. Answer (T) for true or (F) for false to the following statements.

_____ *I provide others with a sense of security.*

_____ *There is always a better way or more than one way to get things done.*

_____ *I am a "big picture" thinker. I see what others can't see.*

_____ *My ideas surprise others.*

_____ *People ask me, "What do you think?" on a regular basis.*

_____ *I freely share my creative thoughts.*

_____ *Others look to me for direction.*

_____ *I give advice freely.*

_____ *I often have already thought of an idea before someone else brings it up.*

_____ *I am clear about the direction of my life.*

_____ *I am clear about the direction of my career or vocation.*

_____ *I effectively lead others towards a shared vision.*

_____ *I frequently receive positive feedback for my thinking outside of the box.*

_____ *I often seek new ways of achieving my goals.*

_____ *Others can easily see and describe what I value.*
_____ *I am willing to risk being criticized for having a vision.*
_____ *I am not afraid to say what I think in a group.*
_____ *I frequently have a different opinion than others in my group.*
_____ *I know I will do great things with my life and leadership.*
_____ *Others' opinions belong to them.*

Interpretation: Count the number of true responses. If you had 15 or higher, it's fair to say you are perceived as a visionary thinker. Others recognize you as such and look to you for guidance. You are respected for not going along with the majority opinion. If you had ten to 14 true, you are perceived as a team player; but resist going against the majority opinion. Be careful about confusing consensus building with good decision making! The charismatic leader is always willing to verbalize in a clear, straightforward fashion, when a group is moving forward and when the group has strayed off course. Don't be afraid to risk being right! Take more chances. If you had less than ten true responses, spend thinking about where you want your life and leadership to go. This book will help!

Many leadership experts identify the ability to "clearly articulate a vision for the future" as the one differentiating trait between effective leaders and exceptional leaders. The research on charismatic traits and follower effects by Conger and Kanungo support these conclusions. "Charismatic leaders differ from other leaders by their ability to formulate and articulate an inspirational vision and by exhibiting actions that create an impression that they and their mission are extraordinary."[1] To have vision is to think above and beyond, which will also require you to be skilled at communicating your goals, mission, ideas and how you see the future, so it is easily understood.

Attributes of Visionary Thinkers

Free Thinking

Free thinkers are magnetic because they see something others don't or have chosen not to see. They think outside the box while others color inside the lines. They create new ways of approaching a desired outcome by examining what needs to be accomplished. They are not only free thinkers; they are free to think. Give yourself permission to direct a desired outcome by envisioning that outcome with enthusiasm. What do you want to see?

Proactive Thinking

Visionary thinkers anticipate obstacles in advance. If you know who will resist your efforts, what resources will be needed, what policies might interfere with your plans, you can incorporate the overcoming of them in your planning process. Weight Watchers has a saying, "Planning prevents pudgy people." It is based on the well documented benefit of thinking ahead of time where, when and what you will have to eat so you can bring snacks, stop ahead of time for lunch or eat the right foods. This approach is effective in helping members overcome potential obstacles and stay on track. It prevents spontaneous overeating, and ensures the right foods will be consumed (and the right amount of points.) With vision comes the need to address challenges before they arise, and set yourself up to be at your best at all times. You never know what can happen! As corporate icon and talk show host Oprah Winfrey suggests, "Luck is a matter of preparation meeting opportunity." Be ready.

Risk Taking

Go beyond the safety nets of what others expect to hear and engage them in a fantasy you intend to make reality. The more you talk about it, the more real it becomes. Continually talk about your vision until it sounds like it already exists. Along the way, there will be decisions to make. Much like being a college student, or new mother, until you've done it, you've never done it. Despite the many books you can read on the subjects, there's no substitute for learning as you go. Said another way, there's no replacing the excitement of taking the necessary risks, venturing out into the unknown, or throwing ideas against a wall to see what sticks! You may fail; we all fail. If you don't risk success, you have guaranteed failure. In *The Wizard and the Warrior*, Lee G. Bolman and Terrence E. Deal make the argument "leaders cannot afford to stay on the sidelines and play it safe. Someone has to be willing to stand up and put it on the line." They refer to these leaders as, "wizards and warriors."

Staying Focused

What can you do to keep your "eye on the ball?" Visionary thinkers surround themselves with reminders of what they are trying to achieve. For example, chairman of Starbuck's Corp, Howard Schutlz is described in *Business Leaders and Success* as staying true to his mission by digging his hands into a bin of freshly roasted coffee beans, and then taking a big whiff. The strong aroma revives Schultz's original passion for the business. Schutlz is quoted as confirming, "[Putting my hands in coffee beans] helps me remember how we got started and what we need to sustain, you have to go back to the cause – which in our case is the coffee. It's our love of coffee."

Other ways of keeping your vision in front of you include placing a chart depicting desired earnings on your office wall, a photo of smiling children on your bookcase, or an architectural drawing of a marina you will own and operate. These visionary reminders also serve to reinforce your internal pictures of the end product. Another approach is to literally put a colleague together, design a logo, or create a symbol representing your vision. You can also make a list as my daughter did for the first edition of this book. She wrote the following when she was twelve years old. Remarkably, she has achieved many of the items listed already, although she probably needs to do a second edition, as well.

My Dreams: Both Big and Small
By Kaitlin Elizabeth Denney (Age 12)

Be the president of the United States.

Write and publish a novel by the time I'm twenty-five years old.

Get into my first choice college.

Be a member of National Honor Society.

Travel to a different continent and see how other people in the world live.

Save someone's life in any way.

Be someone's role model.

Inspire someone.

Meet someone I love and marry him.

Learn to appreciate what I have.

Become a novelist.

Make sure the people around me know how much I love them.

Be a creator of surprise.

Help those who need it, whenever humanly possible.

Never hate myself, but always love myself.

Remember what other people think isn't always important.

Be a leader in my own eyes.

Never give up on my dreams.

Exploration: Your Dreams Big and Small

Directions: Use the space provided to make a list of at least ten desires for your life and leadership – cover vocation, relationships, treatment of self or others, and so on.

_____

_____

_____

_____

_____

_____

_____

Believing in Self and Ideas

According to Dr. Tony Alessandra in *Charisma*, "Charismatic people possess a similar, almost childlike faith in their vision and their ability to create change. People will follow leaders whose vision inspire them and make their lives more meaningful." It's not enough to merely wish the homeless fed, a cure for cancer found, or more children taught how to read; you need to visualize your dreams and desires so they turn into obtainable goals and then, you must believe in your ability to make it a reality. This may require you to find likeminded people, partners or other sources of faith in your potential to achieve your goals.

Most importantly, you will need to have an unyielding faith in yourself. Self-confidence is a powerful source of influence and inspires considerable reverence as others wish they possessed it. You will find self-confidence in a variety of ways, one of the greatest is through faith. Believe you were made to leave your fingerprints in a special way, and make the world a better place, and you won't be afraid or fearful. You will have what you need, when you need it. Marlon Smith, author of *Living with Purpose*, insightfully notes the contradiction found in claiming to believe in a Higher Being, yet not trusting the potential outcome of your efforts when he said, "Faith and fear can't exist at the same time."

Resourcefulness

You will be more visionary than your beige counterparts if you can point out more than one way of hitting a target – a target you clearly see in your mind. Your resourcefulness provides others with hope, direction, and enthusiasm for the future. Visionary thinkers frequently ask, "What do I need to accomplish my goals, where do I find what I need, and what do I have to do to get what I need?" They rarely take "no" for an answer, yet will quickly move on to the next option if they did get a negative response. They will also maximize what is at their disposal, every connection, source of funding, and different approach is considered before it is dismissed. If you want to become a visionary thinker, you will have to start asking, "How?" and delete the "if" mentality.

Associates of Visionaries

Millionaire's Round Tables and Success Circles are all the rage! They aren't anything new, rather a more PC way of naming the age old tradition of associating with equally confident and likeminded people who have similar successful track records or who have something significant in common. So ask yourself, "Who wants to be involved with what I am doing?" Also ask yourself, "Whose lead do I follow?" Vision is often shaped by your associations and environments of opportunity. High achievers, for example, attract other high achievers. Underachievers seek out other underachievers. If you want to achieve your dreams, associate with people who achieve their dreams and can help you achieve your vision. Most likely, these aren't people you know and may require you to work harder to get connected. You may have to network in more fitting circles and do a better job of following up with new acquaintances. You know who you know. To take it to the next levels requires you to befriend a new level of associates!

INFLUENCE 4 INITIATIVES

- Think outside of the box for the tasks you have to accomplish today.

- Draw a picture of your future.

- Close your eyes and visualize every hour of your life in five years.

- Continually discuss your vision. Share it with others.

- Keep your vision in front of you.

- Create a "wall board" or visual reminder of one goal.

- Encourage others to articulate their visions.

- Study the great visionary thinkers of the 21st century.

- Ask every child you meet what they want to be when they grow up.

Chapter 13

INSIGHT FIVE
The Transcending of Adversity

*"Life is like a window. Sometimes you have to
look through the pain to see the view."*
- Randolph Macon, college student

When you are a college student, you get to engage in behaviors otherwise thought to be immature by traditional social standards. You get to stay up all night text messaging your friends across the hall. You get to save all of your dirty laundry until vacation time, when you bring it home to mom. When you are a college student, you can think it's acceptable to wear your pajamas to class, greet people you saw two hours earlier with a big hug, and make strange noises in a crowd of like-minded people, provoking unstoppable laughter. Male or female, college students can be rather playful individuals.

The U.S. Census Bureau reports that less than 30% of the United States' population has a two or four-year college degree. However, the idea of "college" is widely understood. College students go to class, do homework, study and graduate. For some, this privilege is assured. For others, it is an unobtainable goal. The roadblocks (or competing forces) preventing millions of Americans from pursuing higher education range from lacking encouragement to lacking financial resources; for many, the forces working against them are insurmountable compared to the resources available to them. During the recent Bush administration, this gap has gotten consistently greater and students are now graduating with thousands of dollars worth of debt. They are behind before they even begin, yet persevere with optimism and hope in their future.

Adversity is challenge. It represents a powerful or competing force of resistance to you or your mission. Adversity comes in many shapes and sizes. Sometimes we create the adversity in our lives. Other times, adversity happens. Adversity can be real or perceived. Either way, it represents that which you haven't conquered in one form or another, yet must to move forward and bring Zing! to your life and leadership. Examples of adversity include: losing your job, lacking start up capitol, being diagnosed with cancer, growing up poor, losing your eyesight, lacking a supportive family, discrimination, ignorance, and taking care of an aging parent or sick child. The adverse conditions make up the competing obstacles found in the Zing! definition. Rich, poor, tall, short, young, or old; to be human is to face adversity at some point in your life.

Not all adversity needs to be interpreted or received as negative. In fact, exceptional leaders are often defined by their ability to turn the adversity in their lives into character-building opportunities. They have learned or accepted the very difficult lesson: They are destined to do great things, change the world and put their life experience to good use. Instead of being ashamed, embarrassed, victimized, or controlled by the difficult (or devastating) events in their lives, individuals with Zing! accept them as part of their history, then use them for enhanced insight and understanding. You can quickly tell when someone "gets it" because they have "lived it."

You can't run away from adversity. It will find you – or someone you love. Caused by natural events completely out of your control, like the devastation of Hurricane Katrina, or the loss of a parent to Alzheimer's, your only option is to find a way to move forward. Without a doubt, Dr. Martin Luther King, Jr. is one of history's most influential and charismatic leaders. He knew well how those he served struggled on a daily basis due to discrimination, unfair economic practices and institutionalized oppression. It's not by chance he chose the phrase, "We shall overcome!" as a means of communicating not only understanding, but as a source of inspiration.

The internal dilemma of dealing with adversity is under your control. Whether in the form of a significant obstacle, challenge, struggle, physical disability, personal tragedy, national crisis, loss, or lack of opportunity, adversity forces you to make decisions. You have to decide what you are going to do about your situation, how you are going to move forward and where you will find the courage. Overcoming adversity begins with a choice to move forward. The story below is about someone very special. She had every reason not to do great things, yet overcame a host of obstacles to serve the greater social good as a remarkably gifted teacher and minister.

Learning and Teaching for a Greater Good

You cross paths with people all the time and never really know them. You might get the benefit of someone's life experience (the good and the bad) without knowing how (or why) he or she is able to influence the world in such a positive and extraordinary way. One remarkable woman I've had the honor of getting to know is a very intelligent and caring single parent of two, teacher, and licensed minister. From the outside you see confidence, commitment, excellence, talent, and compassion. You see an incredible ability to counsel others and teach not only subject, but life, to her students, colleagues, and community members.

What you don't see is her life story filled with adversity (the catalyst for her understanding and insight). As a child, this women experienced many significant hardships. When she was celebrating her sixth birthday, her eleven year old brother was killed by a drunk driver on his way to school. Soon afterwards, her father was seriously injured on the job, and consequently, her family of thirteen experienced going from middle class to poor. During this time she was also sexually molested.

In her adult life, this influential difference maker overcame significant attitudes and prejudices against female pastors, divorce, economic pressures forcing her to work three jobs to support her family, jealousy, self-doubt, and physical and mental exhaustion. How did she find her way to inspire so many? Despite being tracked in remedial English in 8th grade (because of her sibling's academic reputations), a teacher noticed her intellectual ability and encouraged her to pursue her intellectual development. Her academic confidence built throughout high school. She faced the desire (and ability) to go to college for Elementary Education without *any financial assistance and a discouraging high school guidance counselor. From college she studied in seminary school (where she faced additional discrimination) and became a full-time public school educator. Her goal is to pursue a Master's and Doctorate degree in Educational Leadership and/or Counseling.*

After learning of the adversity my friend has overcome in her lifetime, I asked her how she defines "success" and "happiness." She said, "Success is when the words spoken about you or the thoughts remembered about you are lovingly passed around while eliciting the same intensity of warmth and respect they first created." Her next response speaks to her understanding of adversity, "Happiness is being content in any given situation. When I am in a difficult challenge… I am assured and content that it will pass. This realization enables me to live beyond the boundaries and expectations that can influence my actions and reaction to a given situation."

Exploration: Obstacles to Overcome

Directions: Review the list of potential obstacles below. Place a check mark next to those you believe represent competing forces in your potential to positively influence others. After you have identified these areas of adversity, ask yourself, "How can this be used to my advantage?"

Limited financial resources
Absence of a support network
Time constraints
Poor health or fitness
Family obligations
Discrimination
Low (but growing) self-confidence
Unresolved conflict
Abusive relationship(s)
Lack of education
Emotional scares
Fear of the unknown

Defeatist attitude
Out of control ego
Inexperience in leadership roles
Victim of natural disaster
Single parenting
Care taking responsibilities
Lack of skills
Track record of failure
Harmful addiction
Lack of guidance
Personality clashes
Chip on your shoulder

The Common Bond of Adversity

Did you check off at least one of the above? You most likely did because very few people in this world escape adversity; we just meet our daily challenges and overcome our obstacles differently. My adversity might seem insignificant to your adversity because my life has been different than your life. To become overwhelmed, or resort to ineffective coping mechanism (substance abuse, inflicting abuse on others, withdrawing socially, and so on) when adversity knocks at your door, is to deny the fact: life is difficult. These three words are also the first three words in M. Scott Peck's bestseller *A Road Less Traveled*. Throughout his book, Peck paints an insightful picture of life containing a series of highs and lows. To ignore the lows makes it hard to celebrate the highs.

Likewise, I know from my own experience that not experiencing adversity until later in life leaves you limited in your emotional response set. I was blessed to grow up never having dealt with significant adversity until my husband's cancer. I hadn't had any "practice" using the Insight of Adversity, so I fell hard and fast. It took me a considerable amount of time and effort to recapture a sense of emotional stability. The experience taught me you can't tell someone, "Everything will all be OK," because you don't know that. It also taught me the validity of the following statements: Bad things happen to good people, and Life isn't fair. It is in the handling of adversity that your ZQ either rises or falls. The presence of adversity is predictable and represents competing forces in the Zing! Impact equation.

Overcoming adversity requires you to accept that which you can't change and change the things you can. It also underscores the power of courage, determination and faith as demonstrated in the story above and in the following examples: Early in her career, Oprah Winfrey had to overcome being a victim of child abuse to become a television reporter. President of Meredith College, Dr. Maureen Hartford, had to overcome being a woman in a predominately male field to become one of a handful of high ranking female CEOs in higher education. Professor Dr. Joe Martin had to overcome being told he wasn't "college material" to become one of the youngest college professors in the country. Children's author and president of Alternatives in Motion, Johnny Tuitel, had to overcome what the world considered "normal" or "perfect" to marry the woman of his dreams, and father three great kids despite his physical disability.

Responding to Adversity

The following grid was created to put the complexities of adversity into perspective and suggest how to respond. You begin the process by determining whom or what created the adversity, followed by identifying when it was created and conclude by considering which of the four response strategies is the most helpful to your situation.

The Grid of Adversity

Who Created the Adversity?

IN YOUR CONTROL (CHOICES YOU MAKE)	OUT OF YOUR CONTROL (LIFE)
TIME FRAME: PAST	TIME FRAME: PAST
You leave an argument unresolved.	*A parent/ significant other abandon you.*
You quit your job.	
You spend more money than you make.	*Your company is downsized.*
You do not exercise.	*Credit card interest rates climb.*
You move away from home.	*You are born with diabetes.*
	Your house burns down.
RESPONSE= MANAGE ADVERSITY	RESPONSE= ACCEPT ADVERSITY

IN YOUR CONTROL (CHOICES YOU MAKE)	OUT OF YOUR CONTROL (LIFE)
TIME FRAME: PRESENT	TIME FRAME: PRESENT
Fear of commitment	*Your parents' divorce*
Failure to communicate with your boss	*Corporate culture*
Living over your means	*Cost of living*
Being overweight and out of shape	*Rising medical expenses*
Significant credit card debt	
RESPONSE = ELIMINATE ADVERSITY	RESPONSE = INSURE AGAINST ADVERSITY

Response Strategies to Adversity

MANAGE YOUR EXPOSURE

The source of your adversity is you. As a result of something you did, said, created, or believed in the past, you are still letting the adversity control you! The past isn't going anywhere, but you can! By continually improving your communication skill-set, for example, you can be better equip yourself to effectively listen, confront, manage conflict, and articulate your vision. You should spend time figuring out where you went wrong and what, if anything, you need to do to regain a sense of control over your destiny. If possible, bring closure to unresolved conflicts. If they aren't resolvable, learn to let them go! Don't continually blame others for your shortcomings. This behavior turns people away from you instead of making you more influential in their eyes.

TRANSFER YOUR EXPOSURE

Are you good at letting those who truly care about you, do so? When situations arise that are not of your own doing, seek a greater faith. Live one day at a time, and give yourself time to process the challenges of the past. Often, feelings of helplessness arise when recovering from adversity. Be willing to ask for help. Seek counseling. Reduce the various sources of added pressure in your life until you are in a better position to handle them. Another strategy is to practice forgiveness. Individuals with Zing! are not angry, resentful, unproductive, depressed, or withdrawn. They don't lash out, have highs and lows, or sabotage others' good intentions. The best lesson adversity teaches us is how to handle it with grace.

ELIMINATE YOUR EXPOSURE

When the adversity reflects unfinished business on your part, relationships that bring you down, inadequate health and fitness, low self-esteem, or a fear of taking risks, it's time to either fix the problem, or once again, let it go. Move on! You can't recreate or change the past, so focus on the present. Work through the consistent patterns of dysfunction, failed relationships, unhappiness, stress and poor job performance, or lack of opportunity – they aren't the cause, they are the result. Remember, you are the one common denominator in the equation. Do what you need to do to improve your skills, adjust your attitude, get back in shape, and have a higher sense of self-worth. If you constantly have adverse situations in your life and leadership, look in the mirror. Eliminate your exposure. Turn the wrong into a right.

INSURE AGAINST EXPOSURE

Put strategies in place to assist you in dealing with situations currently out of your control, as well as those that might suddenly arise. As noted previously, charismatic individuals take a proactive approach to life instead of being reactionary.

Be willing to adjust your priorities, think differently, and be comfortable with risk-taking. Continually surround yourself with competent individuals who bring you up and reinforce positive qualities. Distance yourself from those who are toxic, lazy, disingenuous, self-serving and ego maniacs. Go for quality of relationships over quantity. When you provide support for others, they will most likely return the favor. Building a support network before you need one ensures you'll have what you need when you need it.

Insight 5 Initiatives

- Deal with your adversity. Don't ignore it or hope it will simply disappear.

- Yell "Help!" when you need it.

- Seek professional counseling when you need support.

- Be willing to let your friends, and loved ones, love you.

- Record what your adversity has taught you.

- Make a list of the challenges you've already overcome in life.

- Look around. How much do you really know about the adversity your neighbors, friends, and colleagues have overcome?

- Go to motivational lectures or read motivational books.

- When you drive, put in a motivational CD.

- Hug strangers if they look like they need one.

- Hug your friends and family more.

- Read the Prayer of Serenity: Lord, grant me the serenity to accept the things I cannot change, courage to change the things that I can, and the wisdom to know the difference.

INSIGHT SIX
The Curiosity of Courage

*"Far better it is to dare mighty things, to win
glorious triumphs, even though checkered by failure,
than to take rank with those poor spirits who neither enjoy
much nor suffer much, because they live in the gray
twilight that knows not victory nor defeat."*
- Theodore Roosevelt

As a child, I always thought Lassie was simply asking for
a bad day by hanging around Jimmy so much. Episode
after episode, this beautiful dog jumped into garbage dumpsters,
crawled down dilapidated wells, and climbed up cliffs loaded
with mud – all for Jimmy, who couldn't stay out of trouble. If
Lassie could do all those things (as well as climb a ladder) you'd
think she was smart enough to recognize a walking disaster when
she saw one. Jimmy was going to keep getting into trouble,
and Lassie was going to keep saving him. I used to yell at the
television, "Run, Lassie, run! Get out while you can!"

Curiosity and courage are often difficult to separate. Children are born with both. I'm not sure which one we lose first as we grow up. When you observe individuals with Zing! you sense both are still intact. To increase your ZQ, you need to keep (or get back) a youthful curiosity and openness to experiment, create, and navigate new waters. You need to be willing to go where others haven't gone or continue reaching for happiness even when bad things happen to good people. You can't always "play it safe" or "stay the party line." You influence others by daring to blaze a path for others to follow. You achieve the unexpected, surviving where others might not.

Courage is the ability to pull from deep within to overcome something you (as opposed to someone else) view as more powerful. For example, one needs courage to overcome a drug habit (i.e. addiction), leave an abusive partner (i.e. dependency), care for an elderly parent that you know is no longer taking care of you (i.e. security), and to not cheat while everyone around you is cheating (i.e. peer pressure). Courage allows you to rise above whatever is holding you back with the goal of moving forward. It is taking action when others retreat. Courage is not recklessness, however. It is bravery when others are frozen in fear, doubt or lost in self-pity. This doesn't mean individuals with Zing! are never afraid or have legitimate reasons to be sad. In fact, anxiety is a very natural emotion accompanying risk or potential danger, and sadness is a healthy response to loss. To have courage is to accept your fears (and their companion emotions) and move on. To quote Ernest Hemingway, "Courage is grace under pressure."

How would your life be different if you had courage? Is this possibly what's holding you back from achieving Zing! and achieving happiness? Acting courageously nets both positive and negative consequences. On the positive side, courage allows you to survive. Courage also allows you to advance a cause, challenge your assumptions, achieve extraordinary accomplishments and approach controversy productively and constructively. Your ability to move forward, overcome the odds, or resist temptation is rewarded with the knowledge you are setting an example and help those around you to put their own lives in perspective. Although not your intention, your ZQ is raised when you resist fear and act courageously.

In the absence of courage, you risk losing control over your destiny. Courage allows you to ask for help, seek counseling or guidance, and learn what you need to know to get what you want. One of the greatest benefits of courage is learning the value of believing in your potential to screw up, mess up, make up, and move on. With courage comes the ability to color with the crayons life gives you – except for the beige one, and rewards you with the admiration of others. Acts of courage inspire strength and internal optimism. Whether you realize it or not, your courage is a sign of your faith in the future. You give others hope.

You have the potential to give others fear, too. It's possible you may meet (or already know) those who aren't as impressed by your increasing potential to advance your vision simply because your courage brings their inadequacies, fears, and defenses to the surface. This doesn't mean you don't have Zing!, it means your courage may threaten them. In addition, your newly found ability to turn stumbling blocks into stepping stones, set your sites higher then others believe possible, and leave your unpleasant past behind you, might be (and often is) interpreted as "reckless," or creates distrust in your competency. You might lose a few friends for your acts of bravery, be the source of town gossip, and, for no fault of your own, start something that gets out of your control. You will prove people wrong about you, which may or may not be met with appreciation.

Because courage can take many forms, the price you'll pay for being courageous also takes many forms. Telling a bully to leave another kid alone, challenging the amount of alcohol a friend consumes, forcing someone into rehab, or reporting your concerns about the conduct of a high school coach to the principal, are all acts of courage which may result in losing favor in someone else's eyes. Your every move might go under the microscope. You might get called names, talked about or have your intentions questioned by those you thought were "friends" or advocates of doing the right thing. Ask yourself, "In the scope of life, does my intervention make a difference?" If the answer is, "Yes," than accept the consequences.

People with courage can live with the consequences of doing what's right over what's popular. It's not that the consequences don't matter, but to not act would have been the far greater tragedy. Consider the lives and leadership of the following: Nelson Mandela, Dr. Martin Luther King, Jr., Challenger astronauts (1986), Columbia astronauts (2002), Ellen DeGeneres, Arch Bishop Romero, and the passengers who rushed the cockpit to overcome the terrorists and crash their own plane into the fields of Pennsylvania (September 11, 2001). Never expect great things without a great price tag.

Types of Courage
There are two types of courage; sustainable and instant. Lassie (the dog) had all kinds of courage, but had to rely on instant courage the most. She was forced to act immediately or life was over for Jimmy. She displayed what I call instant courage. This is the kind of courage that shows up unexpectedly. You don't have time to think too hard or long about your response, and afterword, are rather impressed with yourself because "you didn't know you had it in you!" Examples include your immediate reaction to emergency situations, "final straws," preventing potential harm to others, or "teachable leadership moments." Not all acts of instant courage are acts – sometimes, not doing something on the spot

takes Zing! like when you hold your tongue or intentionally don't respond because you are too angry.

The other second type of courage is sustainable courage which requires significant amounts of sacrifice, diligence, and commitment. It is the hardest kind of courage because it requires an enormous amount of physical, emotional, and spiritual energy expended over an extended period of time – including a life time. Louisa May Alcott once said, "I am not afraid of storms for I am learning how to sail my ship." Sustainable courage is exemplified: when a single mother takes five years taking night classes to advance her education with the goal of being able to properly take care of her three children; when a teenager repeatedly turns down drugs and stays home instead of going to high school parties where he/she knows there will be drinking and drugs; and when family members spend years traveling around the country to share the story of their precious daughter or sister taken by a disturbed classmate during the Columbine shootings.

As a parent, I can't imagine what it would be like to lose one of my children. How would I get out of bed in the morning? Those who do, and go on, are remarkable people. When they have every reason to give up, they still get up. They carry within them a great insight into the strength found within and frequently, through their faith. They are unaware of how their very presence inspires, teaches and reinforces the power of prayer – proving the special occasions where Zing! is achieved unintentionally. One of my best friend's son, Eddie Urbanowski, passed away from Leukemia on October 26, 2003 at the age of twelve. The eulogy my friend gave her son, as well as, the way she delivered it, summarized the courageous way she and her family had approached the past four years of his life. Speaking not of what she and her family had lost, but rather what they had gained because of Eddie's life, my friend reminded a crowded church what it meant to have sustainable courage, faith and love.

INFLUENCE 6 INITIATIVES

- Be willing to ask What if… followed by Why not?

- Make a list of the ten most courageous people you know.

- Answer: What act of courage are you considering?

- Look for role models who do what you dare to do.

- Follow around and observe those you consider courageous.

- Read a book on Nelson Mandela.

- Go bungee jumping in Australia.

- When you don't find role models doing what you dare to do, do it anyway.

- Make a list of "bragable" moments of courage.

- Get good at taking risks by practicing.

- Change what you can change.

- Check your life's baggage at the door.

- Build a "Dig me" wall highlighting your courageous feats.

- Continually seek new opportunities to develop and pursue your true passions.

Chapter 15

INSIGHT SEVEN
The Plus of Adaptability

*"Imagination is more important than knowledge.
Knowledge is limited, whereas imagination
embraces the entire world – stimulating progress,
giving birth to evolution."*
- Albert Einstein

The most sophisticated summarization of adaptability came to me while having a conversation with a former graduate school classmate. I enthusiastically discussed my latest book project and mentioned how "adaptability" consistently ranked among the top characteristics of highly motivated individuals, charismatic leaders, and well-adjusted people. She humbly responded, "Oh, the Gumby Phenomenon." In the absence of an intellectual response, I simply blurted, "Huh?" Our conversation continued as I tried to sound smarter than my last comment. It was pointless because my friend made the true point, "Adaptability is your ability to bend, stretch, squeeze under doors, reach high, go low, and transform your molecular composition into different states – just like Gumby." I stopped talking.

The opposite of rigid, *adaptability* is the ability to adjust to your surroundings and anticipate environmental changes. It allows you to put in place flexible systems or "upgradeable" mechanisms of dealing with innovation, transition and "the new and improved" rather than being forced to react. In 540 BC, Heraclites made the following comment which applies today, "There is nothing permanent except change." Adaptability requires you to assimilate information, and necessitates the learning of information normally not of interest. Furthermore, it requires sharpened skill-sets of communication, planning, organization, energy optimization, and creativity, to name a few. Not only does your intellectual capability expand with adaptability, but your reliance on others to "give me the projections" or "tell me where I'm going" also diminishes. Influential individuals figure out their direction by using trustworthy information, a clear understanding of past practices, conversations with reliable sources, and their own deductions.

Is it possible being adaptable means knowing more than you want to learn? To illustrate this point, ask yourself, "If the room was on fire right now, would I know how to get myself to safety?" Most likely, you took notice of the large EXIT signs upon your entrance, or would instinctively remember to "stop, drop, and roll," like you were taught as a child. Whether you realize it or not, you already had a strategy mapped in your brain in the event of a fire. You did this out of habit and out of your natural instinct to survive. Do you take this approach in all aspects of your life and leadership?

The need for change exists because change exists. Whether you want to adapt isn't the issue. You must adapt and prepare for change; otherwise, you become extinct or risk harmful consequences. Survival of the fittest is the number one reason to adapt and change with your environment. The number two reason is that you'll be lots more fun. You can't possibly expect to Zing! if you become devastated every time a new person is hired, it rains when the forecast said sunny, or your child gets a new girlfriend. The Dali Lama said, "There is no present. There is merely the past interfacing with the future."

Indications of Being Rigid or Non-Adaptable:

- Consistently resisting or speaking against change;
- Sabotaging those who risk self-improvement by speaking negatively of them;
- Complaining about any and all new systems, policies, or changes;
- Appearing disorganized or flustered over minor changes to your schedule;
- Consistently looking as if you are playing catch-up, paying bills late, or running late;
- Rarely subscribing to resources related to advancements in your field or area of interest;
- Speaking frequently about the "way things used to be";
- Keep bragging about your new 8-Track cassette player;

Adaptability for the Fun of It

I once gave an entire keynote speech for a state conference in a parking lot standing on a chair. The conference center was experiencing "difficulties" with their air conditioning system. Consequently, the fire alarms consistently went off. At one point, in an attempt to re-wire the air conditioning system, an electrical short occurred causing an actual fire. As I quickly jumped off my chair to let the fire trucks through, I pulled from my "imaginary speaker survival skills handbook" the skill of adaptability and humorously taught the audience how to "stop, drop, and roll!"

One of my favorite and fun books on change is *Who Moved My Cheese?* by Spencer Johnson. It's a simple story about two mice and two humans who are challenged to make it through the "maze of life" in search of their cube of cheese (i.e. success, happiness, and goal achievement). The humans, of course, exert lots of initial energy and get to their cheese quickly. And, like most humans, they become comfortable, complacent and call it "home." The mice, however, keep their sneakers with them at all times. They keep accessing the amount of cheese left and predict how long it will last. Before it's too late, the mice – not distracted by all the materialistic accumulations the two humans have put in their new home, move on to find a new source of cheese. Clearly the mice understood the ins and outs of a maze. The mice were willing to leave their zone of comfort and were prepared to consistently move and make adjustments. Who do you think survives?

Similar observations can be said of groups, organizations and entire corporations. Those who keep their sneakers on will stay profitable, dynamic and responsive while those who misread the changing landscape, fail to do market research, and fall behind in technological advances will go hungry. Be looking for the cheese! Be looking to see if your groups, organizations and corporations are progressive because they are adaptable. Indicators more people are walking around in slippers than sneakers include: frequent leadership turnover, inadequate transitional strategies, systems prohibiting adequate exchange of information, inadequate recording mechanisms or archiving, lack of value placed on organizational creativity, conversations circle back to tradition for tradition's sake, goal setting and visionary thinking are not valued, absence of leadership training opportunities, mob mentality or group think as a decision making practice, job insecurity prevails and there is a lack of upgrading technology.

Whether an organization or an individual, man or mouse, you can't ignore advancing technology and the role it plays in your ability to succeed through influence. I knew it was a bad sign when the tech support for Dell started laughing after I asked about buying an extended warranty on my three-year-old laptop! He said it wasn't "worthy of warranty." Within three years I had become a victim of the rapid pace in which technology influences our lives. That was then. Today, the electronic devices of communication are changing at such an incredible rate and becoming more and more multi-functional, you will soon have no excuse for not knowing information almost instantaneously or not immediately responding to someone's email. From now on, others believe you to always be accessible and able to meet their needs within moments! Your failure to meet these expectations (regardless of how unrealistic) may result in others finding you unresponsive, uncaring or inconsiderate. Pulitzer Prize winner Thomas L. Friedman takes an in depth look at Internet Age in his bestseller, *The World is Flat* and makes an argument for a more pro-active response in our society like re-thinking how we think!

Another Tack
By Lilburn Harwood Townsend

"When you suspect you're going wrong,
or lack the strength to move along
With placid poise among your peers,
because of haunting doubts or fears:
It's time to for you to shift your pack,
and steer upon another tack!

When wind and waves assail your ship,
and anchors from the bottom slip;
When clouds of mist obscure your sun,
and foaming waters madly run:
It's time for you to change your plan,
and make a port while yet you can!

When Failure opens your luckless door,
and struts across the creaking floor;
When Fortune flees and leaves your air,
and former friends but coldly stare:
It's time for you to take a tack,
and show the world you're coming back!"

Rigid Consequences

When someone says to you, "I'm not sure you are management material," or "You're not a team player," or "You aren't the type of person who would be interested in …" consider the possibility that you are politely being told, "You are not adaptable!" Failure to be adaptable quickly becomes an Individual Detractor, and will lower your ZQ. Be warned! People will move on regardless of the time it takes you to "get on board." When new information or a new approach is suggested, instead of immediately reacting with a negative comment or criticism, show enthusiasm and be open to possibility. You don't have to agree, but you do need to show consideration towards those who are proposing something new and different. Doing so will show others that you are not fearful of change and that you neither doubt your own abilities nor lack the intelligence or skills to accommodate to something new.

The Process of Change

How do you respond to change? When faced with the need to be more adaptable, are you inclined to respond rationally or emotionally? Under what circumstances are you more willing to "go with the flow" and when do you hold your ground? Similarly, when trying to get others to work together towards a common vision, how do you work around typical responses to change?

Clearly people become apprehensive, uncomfortable, unpredictable, or excited when presented with something different. They also become angry, frustrated, or proceed with cautious optimism. You might have experienced all or some of these responses as well. By understanding the predictable set of emotions and responses involved in change, you will not only direct it better, but you will experience it better!

The Denney Stages of Change

CHAOS

The first stage begins with an internal feeling. Difficulty ensues when you know instinctively it's time to adapt or reinvent yourself (or the direction of your company, career, or major), yet others continually resist or disagree. Observe the resistance and chaos around you, but take the lead anyway. Take the initiative.

CLEARING OF ATTITUDES

When you realize the reasons to change or adapt aren't going away, you finally accept the fact you must change - like it or not. Unlike the gut level instinct in Chaos, in this stage, you have an intellectual understanding and reasoning for adapting – it's either change or be changed time (it's Zing! time, too.) Now is the time to talk about the benefits of making adjustments, praise others for their cooperation, and clearly keep your eyes on the horizon. It's also helpful to stop giving credence to naysayers and focus on those who will help move you (and your cause) forward. Keep in mind it's often easier to motivate yourself to change when you don't have a choice. (Mandatory isn't always a bad thing.)

CHANNELING OF ACTIONS

With the decision to change behind you, your energy supply is freed up to actively participate in how the change will happen. This is the time to take inventory of your situation, assess environmental forces, consider member's needs, determine the nature of the needed change, clarifying direction, consider who needs to know what and why, define the rational, identify and anticipate the biggest blockers or obstacles, create a mental and physical "change campaign," and make a decision to commit to the new you or program.

COMMITMENT

You and those around you begin to literally see and feel something is different. Your positive approach and subsequent productivity create energy that fuels more action. It's too late to turn back. You have adapted. You have become better. You are moving others in the right direction. You have achieved Zing! – and, despite those who still block your efforts, you need to take the high road and realize their resistance is no longer your concern. Whether or not you actually hear anyone say anything isn't important, in this stage you can feel confident you have overridden obstacles to positively influence others! You have won someone's favor, but you may never know whose!

CONFIDENCE

In this final stage of change, you clearly have a defined course of action representative of your vision or purpose. You continually adapt and make adjustments without losing sight of what you are in the world to do, or your immediate goals.

Zing!

Being one of the most noticeable attributes of Zing! people, you will finally recognize the role of confidence is drawing people towards your ideas and life. In other words, getting good at change automatically elevates your ZQ!

INFLUENCE 7 INITIATIVES

- Buy a Gumby figurine to put on your dashboard or desk.

- Read adventure books.

- Walk down the stairs on the left side.

- Practice writing with your opposite hand for an entire day.

- Require others to call you a different name for an entire week.

- Play a game: Predict who around you will do what and when.

- When planning for change, clearly articulate your change rationale.

- Once you clearly define the rationale, define the change.

- Anticipate obstacles as you set goals.

- Openly discuss the fear(s) associated with change.

- Reward yourself (and others) for being adaptable.

- Keep living plants in your office or home – they only grow if you take care of them!

- Read *Who Moved My Cheese* by Spencer Johnson.

- Get a different hair cut or style.

INSIGHT EIGHT
The Positives of Attitude

*"No pessimist ever discovered the secret of
stars, or sailed to an un-chartered land, or opened
a new doorway for the human spirit."*
- Helen Keller

If you've ever gotten up on the wrong side of the bed, you understand what can happen when you go through the day like The Grouch from *Sesame Street*. Your poor attitude causes predictable reactions by those around you. You provoke negative emotions (i.e. resentment, frustration, anger, distain, etc.) in others. Instead of working with you, people turn against you. In response to their behaviors, you became further agitated and combative – or withdrawn and unproductive. By the end of the day (and it's been a lousy one) you have no one to blame but the wrong side of your bed. But the wrong side of your bed didn't get up... you did! You got the day you created. To repeat the underlying premise of Zing!: The energy you exert is the energy you attract.

I believe there are only four kinds of people in the world: those who see the glass as half-empty, those who see the glass as half-empty and hate what's left in it, those who see the glass as half-full, and those with Zing! who know the glass isn't all the way full or empty, so they go in search of a water fountain. Attitude is a powerful thing. Keith Harrell in *Attitude is Everything*, writes, "Your attitude dictates whether you are living life or life is living you. Attitude determines whether you are on the way or in the way." So, ask yourself a few revealing questions: When you arise in the morning, are you aggravated by the hole in the middle of your bagel? If sailing on the ill-fated Titanic, would you have been swearing at the iceberg or looking for the lifeboat? More importantly, how would those who know you answer these questions on your behalf? Nothing is as transparent as your attitude. You carry it wherever you go for all to see. Plato once said, "Don't be fooled by the deceiver, when the deceiver is always with you."

A positive attitude clearly arises from the desire to be happy and make others happy. A positive attitude communicates all you need to say about your outlook on life and the potential you have to override competing forces to positively impact others towards a greater societal good. Zing! is simply not possible without a positive attitude. Just because you are hopeful, enthusiastic and optimistic, doesn't mean you can't be realistic and pragmatic. Having a positive outlook on life doesn't require you to sugarcoat bad news, offer superficial praise, or give overly optimistic and unrealistic assessments of situations. People will question your sincerity.

Your attitude is essentially the manner in which you choose to approach your reality. Of all the things in this world you cannot control, your attitude is not one of them. You can change your attitude instantly, as if turning a light switch on and off. You can recognize when your behaviors become Individual Detractors and immediately replace them with behaviors reflective of who you really want to be – in the Zing! crowd. Not only do the people around you deserve this effort, but you deserve it! Do you engage in behaviors reflective of a positive or negative attitude? Appendix B offers a detailed assessment called, A Matter of Attitude. The exploration below distinguishes between positive and negative behaviors.

Exploration: Attitude Check

Directions: Consider the list of behaviors below. Which do you use more often? For each row, place a check mark next to the item others see you doing more often.

POSITIVE INDICATORS	NEGATIVE INDICATORS
Say "Good morning."	*Grunt.*
Ask "How can I help?"	*Ask "What's in it for me?"*
Eat a healthy breakfast.	*Consider coffee and two Advil a meal.*
Laugh at yourself.	*Make fun of others.*
Praise.	*Criticize.*
Work out.	*Freak out.*
Look to create the future.	*Blame your past.*
Optimize your energy.	*Claim to know all the answers.*
Ask lots of questions.	*Lie to self-preserve.*
Speak the truth.	*Carry your baggage wherever you go.*
Set goals.	*Spread rumors and gossip.*
Manage your time.	*Have low self-esteem.*
Speak positively of others.	*Need to control others.*
Have confidence in your abilities.	*Consider yourself replaceable.*
Train other leaders.	*Sabotage others' advancement.*
Say "I'm sorry."	*Say "I'm right."*
Open doors for others.	*Cut in line.*
Don't watch the clock.	*Count down to 5 pm.*
Volunteer.	*Watch T.V. or play video games for hours.*
Read for pleasure.	*Surf the net.*
Take additional coursework.	*Complain about knowledge acquisition.*
Think critically.	*React without knowing the facts.*
Ask for help.	*Fabricate.*

The Connection between Self-Esteem and Zing!

A positive attitude is a direct reflection of your self-esteem. To be more appealing to others, focus on taking responsibility for your actions instead of pointing fingers. When you blame, bash your so-called friends, gossip, criticize other's good work, and so on, you are saying to others, "I'm not worthy." You are demonstrating the only way to build yourself up is to take others down. For example, I know a speaker who has a hard time saying anything nice about his colleagues. All this tells me is how insecure he is behind his ego. When students mock their professors they are actually communicating their own lack of academic preparation and accompanying fears.

Another reason not to point fingers at others is you are expending valuable energy which could be put to better use training employees, encouraging a different approach or resolution, planning social events to connect people, sharing your vision, inviting the opinions of experts, making a difference in the life of a child, or building the esteem of a peer. You really don't have time to focus on the inadequacies of people who could use your support instead of your criticism. In addition, blaming others often gets interpreted as speaking negatively of them – even if that's not your intent. It is the outcome. Charismatic leaders do not speak negatively of others, they only see the good. It's that simple. There are too many holes in the "I just need to vent" defense. Never doubt that when someone speaks negatively in your presence about someone else, they will also speak negatively of you in others' presence. Such transparency will also require you to refute negative talk offered to you and replace it with compliments.

Characteristics of Positive People

As you change behaviors to reflect your desire to be happier, others respond in your favor. You begin to create a cycle of positive energy that gains momentum with every positive response created and received. One of the quickest ways to be positive is to start associating with more positive people. They are the happy ones! They walk quickly down the hallway, as opposed to acting as if every step was at an altitude of twenty thousand feet. Positive people smile and greet you beyond a brief "Hello." Below are four developing examples of potential responses to use when walking past someone you don't know. With each response and action, your ZQ increases.

Verbal Message: "Hello."
Supporting Behavior(s): Nod. Keep on walking.

Verbal Message: "Hello. How are you today?"
Supporting Behavior(s): Smile and brief eye contact. Keep on walking.

Verbal Message: "Good morning. How are you on this beautiful day?"
Supporting Behavior(s): Smile, sustained eye contact, and hand gesture. Slows down to hear response.

Verbal Message: "Good morning. What brings you here on this beautiful day?"
Supporting Behavior(s): Smile, sustained eye contact, and handshake. Stops to respond and possibly offers a follow-up question, introduction, and/or conversation.

The last exchange clearly demonstrates your intent to make the other person feel more worthy in your presence and validated. If you are shy by nature, practice adding actions and words, as suggested above. Grow into it, but be genuine. Practice incorporating new behaviors into your natural style – your goal is to be the most effective you! Other ways to exude a positive attitude include: laughing, smiling, holding eye contact, active listening, walking with a quick pace, wearing cheerful clothing or a fun tie, hugging, good posture, and paying compliments.

Negative attitudes are revealed through a perceived lack of interest, slow manner of movement, and sloppy dress. Speaking too softly, using aggressive language, being condescending or rude, and making statements which clearly lack in sincerity also suggest a poor outlook on life. When you avoid eye contact, sit with slouched shoulders and put your feet up during conversations, you send the message, "I'm not here to play!" Small gestures of disinterest, violent language, and raising your voice, also push people away. Your goal is be a positive magnet!

Influence 8 Initiatives

- Don't hang around people with negative attitudes.

- Play at work and work at play.

- Exercise on a regular basis.

- Learn to say, "No."

- Don't major in the minors.

- Look for ways to make someone's day.

- Pay for the person behind you at the toll booth.

- Sing in the shower.

- Dance in the streets.

- Laugh out loud.

- Give thanks for your day.

- Spend time alone.

- Read inspirational books.

- Use a calendar with inspirational quotes.

- Send yourself flowers.

- Plant a garden.

- Choose happiness.

- Tell someone how great they are – you'll feel great, too.

Chapter 17

INSIGHT NINE
The Magnetism of Praise

"Brains, like hearts, go where they are appreciated."
- Robert McNamara

Wouldn't it be great to get up every morning to a standing ovation? As your feet hit the floor, you hear applause coming from every room, followed by "More! More!" You shower and think to yourself, "I hope there's enough of me to go around today!" Breaking into the only song you can remember before your coffee, your day begins on the right note, "I ain't nothin' but a hound dog!" Your day begins with a chuckle, twist or two, and an enthusiastic, "Elvis has left the building!" as you head for your car slowed down only by the quick wave you return to neighbors standing on their front porches with their Bic lighters high over their heads in your direction. You know you rock!

From giving your professor a standing ovation to sending a thank-you card, you have many ways to make someone's day and enhance his/her sense of self. You raise your ZQ when you project your positive sense of self onto someone else in the form of praise. As a bonus, every kind gesture makes you feel better in return. Therefore, when in doubt about offering someone praise, think of this quote by management consultant and author Ken Blanchard, said: "Good thoughts not delivered mean squat." Increase your ZQ by increasing the frequency with which you offer praise. Specifically, never leave a conversation without leaving your partner with a compliment. The last emotion you want another human being to feel in your presence is joy. Compliments create joy and praise is the heart of kindness.

It takes the human brain 44% longer to register an insult than it does to register a compliment. As social creatures, I attribute this to a natural need to be validated and positively stroked. When receiving an insult, you have to say to yourself, "Wait! I think my very being is being questioned." Up go the defense mechanisms, rationales, and decisions about how to react. A compliment, however, is a smile you give to someone's soul which is easily accepted.

Praise is an expression of positive affect towards another person with the intent of inspiring pleasure and joy. The more creative you are with your praise for someone's effort, appearance, thoughts, existence, and so on, the more meaningful. You can increase how many ways to communicate praise when you formally or informally provide the following:

Ways to Show Praise

Recognition

Letting people know you notice their efforts, ideas, and contributions is referred to as recognition. Showing gratitude for specific and identifiable work is a valuable form of recognition and often grossly underestimated and underused. In *1001 Ways to Reward Employees*, Bob Nelson reports, "Studies indicate employees find personal recognition more motivational than money." Take the time to notice the outcome of someone's effort – regardless of how trivial or tremendous. There are many ways to offer recognition: Award ceremonies, invitations to dinner, congratulation cards, tipping the hotel maid, giving a day off, making a phone call, dropping by unannounced, offering promotions, providing access, making a certificate and publicly praising.

Attention

You always want to have 20/20 vision when it comes to observing the world around you and those in it. You increase your ZQ when you really see other people. Be aware of when you tend to ignore some people but pay attention to others. Does one person get a handshake while another gets a dull, "Hello?" Your goal is to validate everyone in your presence, as opposed to making them feel unimportant, unappreciated, or undervalued. When you converse with someone and look around the room for someone else to talk to at the same time, you send a very clear message to your conversation partner, "You're not good enough." Treat and greet everyone you meet the same way all the time.

Compensation

A most insightful book by Marcus Buckingham and Curt Coffman, *First Break all the Rules*, does a wonderful job of summarizing specific motivational and environmental working conditions leading to desirable business outcomes. These outcomes are similar to those you desire as a person of influence, enhanced personal magnetism and charisma. Using research conducted by the Gallup Organization over the past thirty years, the authors provide powerful support for looking beyond traditional compensation packages as employees' preferred source of compensation. Instead, they offer thirty-four responses, or "themes," directly correlated to the business outcomes of profitability, customer service, and employee retention.

(Not making the list: how much someone gets paid.) Their research clearly suggests the inspirational value in expanding your interpretation of compensation to include: flexible working hours, complimentary refreshment set-up, "extra credit" opportunities, access to special services, occasional complimentary tickets to a show or ball game, information or resources about hobbies or interests, preferred parking spots, priority in office selection, and increased responsibility. How can you "pay" those you seek to lead?

Evaluation

Usually not perceived to be a good thing, evaluation is the process of letting someone know where they stand with the positive result of reducing insecurity and reinforcing the basic human need to know someone is aware of the outcomes of your efforts. Evaluation is best when not kept a secret – especially when it's favorable! Saying nothing at all is often interpreted as negative reinforcement. Whether you are in an official capacity or position to share a "performance review" on a friend, minister, student leader, parent, spouse, sibling, and so on, doesn't mean you shouldn't take the initiative and make their day! I'm also suggesting that you remember: Behavior that gets rewarded gets repeated! Therefore, don't focus on what isn't being done, or what bugs you. Look for the good. Focus on the "steps in the right direction." Your intent is to leave the other person feeling encouraged, appreciated, honored and happy.

When you receive poor service at a restaurant, for example, the "me-focused" person might say in disgust, "I would have left you a bigger tip had you earned it!" The more considerate "other-focused" person with Zing! (who counts having dinner as blessing) would say, "It looks like you had a considerable amount of tables to handle all at once. Although it would have been nice to see more of you, I'm sure it's been a frustrating evening for you. I hope it gets better." This statement would be reinforced with a 20% tip. The end result is constructive versus critical and has a greater possibility of influencing positive behavior.

Interestingly, praise is often thought to be more genuine if offered by a complete stranger. The recipient takes your compliment at face value because he/she believes you to have no ulterior motive or hidden agenda. What's more, your compliment does not stop with the intended benefactor; when you praise publicly, others may hear or witness the interaction. After you are gone, they see the smile on the recipient's face or the instantaneous change in attitude. Consequently, they too are inspired to praise someone they encounter during their day.

INFLUENCE 9 INITIATIVES

- Be creative with the means you use to praise.

- Praise in public.

- Criticize in private – if at all.

- Be timely in sending thank-you cards.

- Send thank-you cards not emails of thanks.

- Avoid saving a reason to give someone attention.

- Conduct daily performance evaluations.

- Avoid the stressful "annual review."

- Look for the good in everyone you meet.

- Notice something new about someone you see often.

- Do a better job of saying, "Please" and "Thank-you."

- Set aside resources for gifts of recognition.

- Pick up the phone and treat someone to your voice.

- Observe how others show appreciation.

- Read books on how to recognize and reward employees.

- Ask those around you how they know someone values them.

- Go to www.redenvelope.com for recognition ideas.[1]

- Keep people "in the loop" as a means of showing you value their efforts.

- Pay a compliment during every conversation.

- When angry at someone, praise them.

Chapter 18

INSIGHT TEN
The Rules of Respect

"Tact is the art of seeing people as they wish to be seen."
- Dr. Micheal Le Boeuf

I love the "down time" I sometimes get on the road. When I find myself in a hotel room after an evening speech, I take great pleasure in sole possession of the remote control. It's mine. I can watch what I want. Reality shows bug me. Not because they aren't reality; because they are unfortunately true characterizations of greed, inappropriate communication, unrealistic expectations, materialism, fantasy, superficial ideals, intolerance, disrespect, violence and in many cases, emotional abuse. It concerns me these types of shows might suggest a standard or encourage replication. Without a doubt *what* you are exposed to impacts your perceptions and consequently, your behavior – including how you treat others. That's why when I possess the remote I click on the less "dramatic than reality" dramas of Desperate, Grey's, Boston Legal and of course, the "Big Daddy" of real life thrill seeking fishermen, *The Deadliest Catch*!

Given a limited opportunity to create what influences your life and leadership, what do you prefer to watch? If your charismatic potential and subsequent leadership ability is going to be influenced by those in your environment, who do you want around you: Greatness or Mediocrity; Average or Fabulous; Zing! or Beige? When others are in your presence, who are they around? To accomplish great things, you need to see yourself as great – it all starts with you. Therefore, when discussing the value in respecting others, you need to examine if you are respectable. If you display anything less than self-respect, for instance, others will see right through your superficial attempts to show them respect. William Hazlitt said, "A man meets with no more respect than he exacts." Possess the positive attributes – like respect, honesty, fairness and consideration – you want to develop in others.

The ability to hold someone in high regard or esteem as demonstrated through interaction is *respect*. Having respect for someone implies you desire to offer them your best all the time; not because someone (or something) is forcing you; rather you sincerely believe they deserve it and are worthy. You genuinely care about the welfare of others; those you know and those you don't know (referred to as unconditional positive regard.) You are able to care about others because you aren't wrapped up in yourself.

How to Demonstrate Respect

Appearance

One of the most obvious indicators of respect is how you choose to appear in someone's presence. Your appearance should reflect what you are trying to accomplish in a specific environment and the message you want to send about your personality, priorities, purpose and presence. Therefore, your attire, attention to grooming and overall appearance needs to be more of a priority than if you are merely looking to hang out with friends, be a high student, pick up the mail or walk your dog. With regards to appearance, however, it's not really about fashion, designer names or the latest trends, as much as, it is about the non-verbal message being sent. You want your appearance to reflect a concerted effort, something you spent time on in honor of others.

For instance, I chuckle and frown when watching college students wear their pajamas to class. They have misinterpreted their learning environment as one of casual or passive. Instead of showing their professors the respect they have clearly earned, they put their own comfort first. This inconsideration goes mostly unchallenged – unless the professor starts to show up in his or her sleeping attire! There is a disconnect between the student's interpretation of class and having class. A collegiate classroom is not a bedroom; it is a place of intellectual exchange. Albeit comfortable, students in pajamas unknowingly project disrespect to their professors and make a statement of how worthy they are of learning. The same can be said of "dress down" Fridays!

What to wear? As a general rule, consider the Plus One approach to wardrobe selection. When you are being featured at an event, running it or attending an event where you want to make a significant positive impression, find out what others will be wearing and go one step higher. For example, when I walk in a room where I'll be speaking, other people should be able to conclude from my appearance (and behavior) that I am the speaker. Prior to the speaking date, I inquire as to what the audience will be wearing, then dress slightly more formal. I do this out of respect for my audience. A good rule of thumb is to err on the side of being "over" not "under" dressed!

The more casual you dress, the harder it is for others to determine your role, and the greater the assumption by others you might not be taking your role seriously. Appearance is a touchy subject. I know substance matters, as does cultural identity, freedom of expression and the personal choice not to be identified as one gender or another based on attire. I also wish I could say with all certainty, "Clothes do not make the man – or woman." Depending on the situation, they do. Clothes, hair style, cleanliness of attire, personal hygiene, color choice, shoe selection, style of dress, and such, are important to the extent they are important to those you are trying to positively influence.

Communication Methodology

Are you a good communicator? Given all the types and purposes of communication, it takes a considerable effort to effectively express your ideas, listen attentively, articulate your vision, show emotion, and engage others in your journey. To show respect through communication: use appropriate language, speak so you can be heard, minimize distractions, avoid sarcasm, and listen to agree. Don't yell, raise your voice or become violent. Never storm out of a room. Your lack of control might be perceived as disrespect. On the other hand, your need to control might also be perceived as disrespectful. Effective communication seeks not to intimidate, degrade, embarrass, shame, or disrespect – just the opposite.

Word Selection and Gestures

When what you say is inspiring, constructive, intelligent, well thought out and coherent, you communicate the value you place on being understood and understanding others. At the same time, you demonstrate positive regard for the other person's values, morals, and diversity. Out of ignorance comes communication filled with the use of profanity, stereotyping, racist remarks, sexist jokes, and slang. Although some may argue these are integral parts of one's culture, be sure the other person is either of the same culture or agrees. More often than not, your ZQ will decrease with inappropriate word selection and this is a book about influence! Likewise, obscene gestures, winking, slapping someone on the butt, etc. may be perceived as offensive and oppressive and are big Individual Detractors. No doubt about it; leave these out.

Punctuality

The venues or events you attend and when you arrive demonstrate the level of respect you have for the planners and those in attendance. Perpetual lateness is another significant (and preventable) Individual Detractor that subjects itself to a variety of interpretations and/or assumptions about you. When you are late, others may perceive you as: disorganized, rude, careless, inconsiderate, self-centered, distracted, or lazy. A friend told me her boss instilled in her the importance of punctuality by saying, "Early is on time and on time is late!" Zing! requires you to be on time. Stop apologizing! Stop showing up after a one hundred yard dash! Try putting post-its around your space to remind you of appointments, meetings and obligations involving others. Enlist someone to give you a "heads up" or reminder. Get a bigger wall calendar. Do what you need to do to be on time – especially Zing! time.

Scheduling

How you prioritize someone else's time versus your own directly signals their importance to you. Whose time is more important? For example, you may arrive on time, but if you leave early, you have done the same thing as if you had arrived late. It is far better to re-schedule than ignore the fact that someone else, or a group of individuals, made time for you but you did not reciprocate. Cutting a speech short because you have to catch a plane, not eating at a lunch meeting because you have another lunch engagement, or sitting down for coffee without taking off your coat are all subtle signs of disrespect.

Attendance

Did you realize with every missed dinner, weekend trip to the office, skipped class, or failure to show up to your child's recital, you send the message, "You are only worthy of my left-over time." To respect others is to be there. Honor your friendships, family gatherings, volunteer commitments, involvements, and people in your life with your attendance.

Hours of Operation

Given the speed dial function, it's easy to forget to look at the clock before hitting Send! You look up a name on your cell phone wherever you happen to be and forget to consider where the person you are calling might be at that hour. When you reach out matters; avoid unannounced visits during someone's work day. If someone clearly appears to have much on their plate, offer to help or let them get it done instead of enticing them away from their responsibilities because you have some "free" time! Look at your watch before calling someone and consider if it's the appropriate time and day. For example, bosses who call employees on Easter Sunday, show complete disrespect for their employees' personal space, as do those who call all hours of the day, night and weekend.

Involvement

Another very important way of showing respect is by your level of involvement in your workplace, community and relationships. Specifically, what do you support and give your time to coordinate, plan and participate in? When I lived in my former town, I frequently spoke at the local library. I got a kick out of the fact all my friends would show up – and sit in the front row! Although they've heard me speak many times, they still participated, asked questions, and laughed at my jokes. I was honored. I receive the same positive regard from colleagues who despite being capable of giving my workshop presentations, will arrive early and help me set up! Other ways to validate someone's efforts and "tell" them you find them impressive human beings include: Attend a Little League game coached by a colleague; Check out the art show of your friend's sister; Volunteer to chaperone your son's class field trip; Clean up after a program coordinated by your roommate; Help plan a 50th birthday party for a relative; Sit at the sign up table for the Red Cross; Distribute programs on the chairs of your pastor's Bible Study. Before you decline an invitation to contribute, ask yourself, "Is this an opportunity to show respect?"

Solicitation of Opinion

Respect is also demonstrated by inviting others' opinions and participation. When you say, "Can I bounce an idea off of you?" The recipient hears, "You have a brain in your head and I respect your take on this." Have you ever been asked to serve on a committee because someone respects your talents? It's flattering to be invited to do more work! Supervisors who micro-manage show very little trust (and thus, respect) for their employees' abilities. What they project on a daily basis is: You can do this, but I want to check it. To dignify others' talents, opinions, and ideas is to encourage their insight, perspective, and intellectual contribution. Who would be honored to work with you?

High Expectations

Leadership expert Warren Bennis notes, "Great expectations are evidence of great respect." By letting others know your expectations, you are telling them how you perceive them. Just as high expectations of others demonstrate your high esteem, low expectations of others demonstrates your low esteem. When you undervalue, underpay, and under-appreciate those you seek to inspire and lead, you simply disrespect them and in the process end up disrespecting yourself. The same outcome results when you prevent access, limit upward mobility and promotion, or assume a lack of interest in their lives. Honor those you are blessed to serve by believing in their potential.

Politeness

Last but not least! Showing politeness is the humble way of acknowledging the respect and high esteem you feel others deserve. As with all Zing! things, politeness requires putting others ahead of you. It is an indicator of your ability to show basic unconditional positive regard and consideration all the time and to everyone – not only to those you might gain from. Examples of politeness include: not making more work for someone, keeping a room as clean as you found it, verbally stating your appreciation or desires, letting someone go ahead of you, and refraining from being rude. Thank you for reading!

Influence 10 Initiatives

- Respect yourself.
- Establish relationships with people you respect.
- Observe how they treat others.
- Follow through on your promises.
- Arrive 15 minutes early for all appointments.
- Return phone calls within 24 hours.
- Stand up quickly upon seeing someone approach you.
- Stand when shaking someone's hand.
- Give your seat to someone else who needs it more.
- Ask someone how he or she would like to be addressed.
- Use someone's formal name (i.e. Mrs. Jones) unless instructed otherwise.
- When someone else is speaking, listen without interruption.
- Don't take a call when in a conversation.
- Never answer your cell phone when having a meal with someone.
- Turn off your cell phone before a conversation or at a public venue.
- Cover your mouth if you yawn (please!).
- Slow down before approaching a door to let others go ahead of you.
- Hold a door open for someone.
- Refrain from putting your seat back on a plane.
- Offer food or drink to others before you take one.
- Wait until everyone has been served before eating.
- If someone drops something, quickly pick it up for them.
- Buy and read an etiquette book.

Chapter 19

INSIGHT ELEVEN
The Necessity of Nourishment

"He maketh me lie down in green pastures:
he leadeth me beside still waters."
- Psalm 23:2 (kjv)

I sometimes think there just aren't enough boxes of Wheaties cereal to go around. Although the cereal is tasty and a wonderful source of dietary fiber it's the outside of the box that gets my attention. Since 1924, Wheaties has been the official "breakfast of champions," honoring "inspirational role models and champions in their community through their charitable endeavors." The first athlete to grace the box cover was Lou Gherig in 1934. Since then, Bob Richards (1958), Chris Evert (1987), Tiger Woods (1998), and Lance Armstrong (1999) have proudly met the criteria. Forever etched in my mind is the 1977 Wheaties box cover with Bruce Jenner in his red, white, and blue track uniform. I get inspired just thinking about it! This image solidifies the achievement of extraordinary results through physical training, mental toughness, extensive conditioning, and proper nourishment – making the cover of cereal box not withstanding!

Do you have what it takes to be extraordinary? Are you physically, mentally, spiritually and emotionally strong enough to serve a greater social good and achieve happiness? In *The Power of Full Engagement,* Jim Loehr and Tony Schwartz note, "Great leaders are stewards of organizational energy. They begin by effectively managing their own energy. As leaders, they must mobilize, focus, invest, channel, renew and expand the energy of others." If you are perpetually exhausted by the daily demands on your time, consistently ill, or have difficulty coping with stress, you simply don't have enough energy to fuel your own needs, let alone anyone else's needs.

Sources of Zing! Nourishment

The four sources of nourishment for Zing! are categorized as physical, emotional (or psychological), spiritual, and intellectual (or mental). The benefits of nourishing all four sources – as opposed to only focusing on one or two, are numerous because of how they interact. There will be times when the demands on your body leave you not only physically exhausted but emotionally spent. Your tired body will cause you to become irritable, cranky, and lethargic. Likewise, when you find yourself frustrated over your inability to generate new ideas or find yourself emotionally exhausted, you will need to rely on physical movement to re-energize your thinking and feeling capacity. The foot bone is connected to the leg bone!

Physical Conditioning and Care

Taking care of your body speaks volumes about your sense of self. When you take the time to prioritize your health and fitness, you make a noticeable statement about your self-esteem and self-worth. As a result of a regular exercise regime, your ability to resist disease increases while your blood pressure and cholesterol levels decrease, your circulatory system works more efficiently, you release healthier chemicals in your system, and you reduce the harmful effects of environmental stressors on your body while improving your mood.

Exercise is clearly one of the best ways to take care of your mind and body. Maximize your workouts by alternating the kind of exercise you get every week. Most fitness experts recommend you include a weekly regime of weight lifting, aerobic workouts and interval training. If you don't have a regular workout regime, start now! Exercise (especially when it is your first morning activity) kick starts your metabolism for the entire day. Throughout the day, you continue to benefit from a more efficient metabolism.

As recognized experts on energy efficiency, Loehr and Schwartz note, "Because energy diminishes both with overuse and with under-use, we must balance energy expenditure with intermittent energy renewal." Therefore, not only is exercise important, but so is rest. To function optimally, you need seven to eight hours of sleep per night. Additional ways to rest is to take breaks during your busy day, alternate tasks, or stop what you're doing, stretch, change your environment or activity, then return.

Another way of taking care of your body is to not put it in harm's way. Preventative measures such as wearing a seatbelt, good oral hygiene, not driving while you are tired, and having an annual physical, demonstrate the value you place on good health. Eliminate (or don't start) potentially harmful activities like smoking, binge drinking, taking drugs, consuming high energy drinks loaded with caffeine, and irresponsible sexual activity. These will lead to bodily damage, illness, and chronic health problems. You should recognize by now your ZQ goes up when others have confidence in your judgment – especially your personal judgment. Think of the last time you saw someone speed by you doing 100 miles an hour and thought, "Wow, how cool is that! I'm so impressed." In truth, weren't you thinking they could kill somebody?

Healthy Eating

Taking care of your body also means watching what you put into your body. Proper diet plays an enormous role in the way glucose (your body's fundamental energy source) is used in your body. Despite the preponderance of diet theories, food fads, and proposed changes to the Food Pyramid, the most reliable course of good nutrition is to eat in moderation, reduce the amount of unrefined sugars and carbohydrates you consume, increase your water consumption to 8 glasses a day (sixty-four ounces), take a daily vitamin and continue to eat a balanced diet of the right protein, fruits, and vegetables. Eating smaller portions more frequently prevents over consumption at one meal. Limiting your caffeine intake is important and will become less and less necessary as your Zing! increases.

One of the best ways of ensuring your daily endurance is to fuel your body in the morning. Skipping meals (especially breakfast) is like expecting to drive a car a long distance without putting any gas in it. When you skip breakfast, you start your day by running on "fumes." Eat breakfast and take the time to begin every day on the right foot. Not only will this practice give you energy, it will help you to protect against stress.

The ill effects of stress on your body are well documented. Like charisma, stress is in the eye of the beholder. Most people are not disturbed by events themselves; but rather by their opinion or perception of those events. Dr. Wayne Dyer says, "Change the way you look at things, and the things you look at change." You have to "see" an event as stressful for it to have a negative psychological effect on your system. Cumulative effects of stress are so often masked, and/or have become so socially acceptable they are ignored as significant warning signs. Frequent headaches, jaw clinching, gastro-intestinal discomfort, teeth grinding and disruption in sleep patterns, for instance, are the result of your body losing the fight with your head.

Stress doesn't go away; it hides. You must find a way to effectively manage and reduce the harmful effects of stress on your health. Remind yourself, "Don't sweat the small stuff because it's all small stuff" when the need for perspective arises. Effective means of managing your stress also include daily exercise, proper diet, relaxation techniques, counseling, meditation, proper sleep and elimination of the stressors.

Emotional and Mental Health

How you handle your feelings affects whether others will view you as capable or in over your head, optimistic or pessimistic, irrational or rational, and so on. Emotions which earn others' positive regard include the following: patience, self-control, empathy, calmness, joy, emotions that earn others' positive regard – not freaking out. The ability to consciously recognize which emotions you are displaying at any given moment is important because people read emotions before they believe the words being spoken. The tone of your voice, rate of your speech, degree of eye-contact, and non-verbal messages accurately articulate your emotional state. Zing! isn't possible when your words and perceived state of emotion are in conflict.

Spiritual Health

Faith plays a vital role in your happiness. Despite the fact that much of the research I conducted for this book views "spirit" to mean your "inner child" or "sense of adventurousness," I use the term as a source of energy derived from your religious beliefs and faith in a Higher Being. We are not alone in this world. If you don't already have one, seek a source of faith and be open to experiencing the reciprocal peace, comfort, and strength. Mother Teresa said, "Faith keeps the person that keeps the faith."

Some of the greatest difference makers were guided by their faith and weren't ashamed to talk about it. Every speech by Dr. Martin Luther King, Jr., for instance, has biblical references.

Former President Jimmy Carter, openly spoke of the strength and guidance he received from his Master. A strong spiritual energy source allows you to step back and view your life and leadership as it relates to a much larger universe. Pastor John C. Maxwell in *The 21 Irrefutable Laws of Leadership* says, "People cannot give to others what they themselves do not possess." How strong is your faith?

The Language of Faith
By Reverend Robert MacFarlane

The language of the world says, "What's in it for me?"

The language of faith asks, "What's in it for the other person?"

The language of the world says, "Stick 'em up! I want your cash."

The language of faith says, "How much do you need?"

The language of the world fearfully says, "Save my life."

The language of faith boldly says, "Take my life, and let it be consecrated, Lord to Thee."

The language of the world sadly says terribly hurtful words to an aspiring young Rutgers women's basketball team.

The language of faith proclaims, "Precious Lord, take my hand, lead me on and help me to stand."

The language of the world says, "The storms of life are too heavy and too overwhelming."

The language of faith says, "Thru the storm, thru the night, lead me on to the light. Take my hand, precious Lord, lead me home."

Intellectual Health

Use it or lose it! Research has found the more we challenge our brain and stretch it to greater intellectual pursuits, the more we increase our capacity to retain knowledge, assimilate ideas, and recall facts. Loehr and Schwartz point out the additional benefit of mental exercise, "Continuing to challenge your brain serves as a protection against age-related mental decline. The key supportive mental muscles include mental preparation, visualization, positive self-talk, effective time management and creativity." Intellectual stimulation and longevity is well documented, yet we often opt for evening television instead of quiet reading. Turn off the tube and pick up a book – Sudoku perhaps? You must use these muscles or else you will lose these muscles. When was the last time you were impressed by someone who bragged about being stupid or made the statement, "I haven't read a book in over five years!"

Exploration: Fit to Live, Lead and Be Happy

Directions. Given the enormous impact of physical, emotional, psychological, and spiritual nourishment on your ZQ, are you willing to do the work? Below is an inventory of health and wellness indicators. Ideally, the more that applies the better. Check those attributes which are true on a daily basis, and put an asterisk next to those you need to work on. Use the following as a "to do" list if necessary!

_____ *I wake up rested.*

_____ *I have a best friend.*

_____ *I eat a healthy breakfast.*

_____ *I challenge my intellect to learn more.*

_____ *I use stairs instead of an elevator.*

_____ *I know how to prepare healthy meals.*

_____ *I am my ideal weight.*

_____ *I brush my teeth at least twice a day.*

_____ *I floss daily.*

_____ *I get annual dental check-ups.*

_____ *I get an annual physical.*

_____ *I get annual eye exams.*

_____ *I lift weights three times a week.*

_____ *I drink at least eight glasses of water daily.*

_____ *I do not smoke.*

_____ *I don't inhale secondhand smoke.*

_____ *I never drive after drinking.*

_____ *I drink in moderation.*

_____ *I drive within the speed limit.*

_____ *I practice a faith that sustains me.*

_____ *I have a support system.*

_____ *I sleep at least seven hours a night.*

_____ *I eat three servings of fruits a day.*

_____ *I don't take risks with my health.*

_____ *I feel energized and healthy.*

_____ *I stretch at least three times a week.*

_____ *I take a daily vitamin(s).*

_____ *I manage my anger.*

_____ *I am in control of my emotions.*

_____ *I wear a seatbelt in a car.*

_____ *I have no or safe sex.*

_____ *My relationships are respectful.*

_____ *My memory seldom fails me.*

_____ *I avoid dysfunctional relationships.*

_____ *I possess internal strength.*

_____ *I am capable of rational thinking.*

_____ *I can control my emotions.*

_____ *I value taking care of myself.*

INFLUENCE 11 INITIATIVES

- Meditate.
- Take time for self-reflection. Spending time in contemplation is often a wonderful way to prepare for a busy day and anticipate the challenges you will face. Consider the same location every day and at the same time. Pick a peaceful place that allows solitude.
- Write down your thoughts.
- Eat for energy. Go with unprocessed foods whenever possible, bright-colored vegetables, and a limited amount of refined sugars and carbohydrates.
- Adapt a daily exercise regime.
- Alternate the types of exercise you get, from aerobic workouts like walking to swimming.
- Stretch three times a week.
- Lift light weights two times a week.
- Remember: Your body is yours for life!
- Get organized.
- Take a proactive approach to scheduling and delegating.
- Avoid over-scheduling your time.
- Listen to relaxing music.
- Hug more!
- Surround yourself with inspirational materials.
- Read for fun.
- Go back to school.
- Subscribe to a magazine, or pick up the latest bestseller.
- Join a professional association.
- Get a personal trainer.
- Get a dog who likes morning walks.
- Schedule annual medical exams.

Chapter 20

INSIGHT TWELVE
The Draw of Intelligence

"A moment's insight is sometimes worth a life's experience."
- Oliver Wendell Holmes

Having parents who were college professors put a damper on my youthful desires to use slang and improper grammar. At the dinner table, my sisters and I were expected to join the conversation, share our opinions, and debate ideas. Regardless of our age, we were reminded of the importance of facts. My mother used to say, "Without facts, how do you know that what you know is worth knowing?" This upbringing taught me something very important and useful throughout my lifetime: Knowledge is the foundation of thought. What do you know and how can you know more?

How far would you follow someone who knows less than you know? What do you think about people who think way too much about way too little? The value you place on intelligence will be just as important as your applied intelligence when striving to positively influence others. In short, the use of your IQ will positively impact your ZQ and people will find you interesting if you have genuine interests. When you form opinions based upon accurate information, think critically, and are inquisitive, you communicate intelligence. There is a big difference, however, between a big IQ and how you are perceived – or your ZQ! Intelligence is not summed up in a single test score.

Methods for Advancing Your Intelligence

Intelligence is the capacity to acquire information, critically think, employ creativity, compare and contrast information, apply knowledge, use common sense, love learning, incorporate humor and wit, teach, and understand the difference between wisdom and ignorance. The most important of these components is a love of learning. You will always inspire others to do great things if you can demonstrate your continued awareness of – or desire – to learn great things. Benjamin Franklin said, "The only thing more expensive than education is ignorance." You can be perceived as "intelligent" through a variety of means.

Seeking different points of view, as opposed to coming off as "knowing it all" is an indicator you value data, facts, and are willing to arrange and interpret them in their proper perspective to form and understand different points of view. Perspective is often found in history; you must look at more than the present. Points of view are not found in one opinion; you must seek many opinions. Zing! thinkers are sponges who actively pursue a variety of water sources and remain open to numerous opinions because you are secure enough to welcome dissent, as opposed to being threatened by it. You are willing to table votes if there is unanimous agreement because you value (and seek) diverse opinions.

I am a fan of any kind of education. The very reason I wrote this book is to inspire those who can read it to help those who can't read it. Share by teaching and among the many rewards is the message you send about the value of using your aptitudes to show your gratitude! Teaching someone to read requires knowledge and personal time. Do you have time? Mahatma Gandhi said, "We must be the change we wish to see in this world." He used the verb "be" as an expression of action and ownership. Did it occur to you that your intelligence can make all the difference in the world – literally? If you teach one person to read, then you've changed his/her life forever.

There is no such thing as a bad question. Asking questions indicates your desire to collect as much information as you can to make informed decisions, formulate an opinion, and consider various points of views and is a powerful way of being perceived as inquisitive. When you ask questions, you let others know that you value their opinion. Be confident and have courage to ask questions when you don't understand something. Children understand this instinctively and will raise their hands enthusiastically to get the attention of their teacher. When these same children become high school students, they don't want the attention of someone who could help clarify, explain, or direct. Down go their hands. What's changed? It takes Zing! to seek others' counsel – and consider it. Always ask questions in a respectful manner, thus leaving the other person's basic human rights intact. Intimidation, threat, and coercion are Individual Detractors and manipulative means of inquiry.

Take advantage of any means you have to literally get smarter. Knowledge acquisition is designed to enhance your intelligence because it provides the content of life. Gandhi once said, "Live as though you were going to die tomorrow, learn as though you are going to live forever!" Consider carrying a best seller around with you, read the paper every morning, catch CNN, take night courses, go to class, read autobiographies, attend seminars, listen to smart people, go to cultural events, read history books and watch documentaries. Fill your head with information and you will have the knowledge necessary to think!

Traits of Intelligence

Would your coworkers or your peers consider you smart? On what basis would they draw their conclusions? Consider the signals of intelligence below that assess and/or determine your pursuit of knowledge. In most cases, there is a cause and effect relationship!

The books you read. Can you discuss Dan Brown's *The DaVinci Code* with someone you've just met? Have you read any/all of the *Harry Potter Series*? The top ten bestsellers are great conversation starters and demonstrate your love of reading. Which genres interest you – Fiction? Non-fiction? Mystery? Science Fiction? How-to books?

The content of your conversations (including your vocabulary). In other words, what you talk about – and with whom – can greatly increase or decrease your Zing!. For example, racist, sexist, vulgar profanity, and discriminatory comments are blatant signs of ignorance; not intelligence. Show a command of the English language, proper grammar, and an extensive vocabulary.

The media to which you expose yourself. You are what you watch and read. Reading offensive materials will project that you are offensive. When you listen to public radio, you project that you value divergent thinking and world views.

Your associations (or lack of) with other intelligent individuals. Who you choose to call friends, colleagues, and associates will reflect upon you. Seek those who know more than you do and befriend them. Be quiet when they speak.

Reference to world affairs. You have to know about the world to know how you will make it a better place. Talk about politics, world economies, and ideologies. Discussions don't have to be solely based upon your opinion, but they can be lively when you share them.

Zing!

Your ability to grasp new ideas. The speed with which you pick up on new material, thoughts, and ideas suggest your "sharpness."

The level of your participation in conversations. Even if you are shy, try stepping out of your comfort zone and force yourself to make a verbal contribution to conversations. On the other hand, if you tend to dominate conversations you will detract from your ZQ because others will think you don't care about giving them a chance to talk.

Conduct in classes, meetings, or at events. Talking over someone or interrupting is rude and suggests your own self-importance or immaturity. Honor your company by paying attention while they are speaking.

Your ability to recall facts and events. When I was in college, John Dean came to speak about Watergate. I was fascinated by his ability to recollect very specific information and conversations with others. To this day, it wasn't just the content of what he said that impressed me, but rather his ability to remember the details.

Appreciation of the arts. A clear sign of your appreciation for history and culture is your appreciation of the theatre, music, and art. These things represent a common bond among humanity. When you take advantage of the opportunities to enrich your cultural experience, you make a statement about your desire to pursue different subjects and become more enlightened, interesting, and well-rounded.

Put Your Intelligence to Good Use

If you have a brain in your head, use it! It's time to be more creative, inquisitive and pensive. Go ahead and pontificate if you must! Get reflective, introspective and cerebral! You can change the world because you can think. When you combine what's in your head with what's in your heart, you get incredible power!

Nothing is impossible if you literally put your mind to it. The use of your intelligence allows you to overcome a great number of competing forces best illustrated in the following questions:

Isn't it easy to forget about the hungry when you eat more than enough every day?
Isn't it easy to ignore the homeless when you sleep under a roof every night?
Isn't it easy to not hear the cries of abused children when your own children are laughing loudly?
Why don't you have time to put what you know to the service of mankind?

One Person Can Make a Difference

A few years ago, I met a man studying and talking to himself in an airport. I asked, "Excuse me. It's been a while since I've seen such interest in a topic. What are you studying?"

The man replied, "Child advocacy laws."

I followed up with, "Are you an attorney?"

A soft smile came over his face as he said, "I wish."

This comment was followed up by a brief explanation. Apparently my travel partner volunteers for CASA and was trying to learn what he needed to know to best serve the child to whom he'd been assigned.[1] At the end of the conversation, he gave me his business card and boarded the flight. After I got home curiosity got the best of me and I pulled out his business card and discovered the gentleman was the international vice-president for a billion-dollar telecommunications company who was taking the time to apply his intelligence differently from his to work. He made the time to learn about a cause and make a difference.

INFLUENCE 12 INITIATIVES

- Read.
- Refrain from discussing how much you don't know about a topic.
- Express your desire to learn more about a topic.
- Maintain an open mind.
- Validate other people's intelligence.
- Admit when you don't understand something.
- Read.
- Learn another language.
- Travel to foreign countries.
- Study a historical figure.
- Discuss politics.
- Go back to school.
- Read the Additional Reading List.
- Enroll in adult learning courses.
- Audit a course.
- Build your vocabulary.
- Learn about and support a cause.

Chapter 21

INSIGHT THIRTEEN
The Example Setting of Determination

*"Great people are just ordinary people with an
extraordinary amount of determination."*
- Garner Dunkerly, Sr.

It's a bird. It's a plane. No, it's Superman.
I will never look at Superman the same since Christopher
Reeve's horse riding accident which left him physically
challenged and physically unable to leap tall buildings in a single
bound as his character once did. In the remaining years of his
life, he enlisted the support of his celebrity friends and used his
own popularity to bring much needed attention to the continuing
need to support research for spinal cord injuries. This true to
life "superman" succeeded in raising awareness about spinal
cord injury patients' needs, which has resulted in increased
government financial support and advance medical research
efforts. There is still a long way to go. He accomplished this
through an unwavering optimism, strong base of support and
remarkable determination.

Think of those you know personally who you describe as "determined." Consider where they started out and where they ended up. Determination is the drive that got them from point A to point B. It is a force greater than opposing forces. It creates momentum and keeps your life and leadership moving forward. Leadership without momentum is like sailing without wind. You can blow into your mainsail (I have personally tested this theory) all day, but you're still not going anywhere because it's just not enough air. Like sailing, once you begin to move others toward a desired destination, you begin a process that sustains itself with less energy than it took for you to stand still.

Reflecting your ability to make a decision and act accordingly, *determination* is a sense of certainty, strength, and direction. To have determination is to be void of uncertainty, "flip flopping," indecision, and/or circumstance. At times, determination has the same charismatic outcome as a clearly articulated vision or purpose; it not only fuels the means to an end, but is a desired attitude in and of itself. The great thing about determination is you don't always need to know exactly where you are going or exactly how you will get there. If you can communicate an unyielding belief or confidence in your abilities to move forward, others will have faith in your potential. If you've ever commented about someone, "That person is going places," then you understand the influence of determination.

Characteristics of determined individuals include the ability to stay on task, or focus. You literally say "No!" to distraction and stay your course. You get up after you get knocked down. You take advantage of opportunities to achieve your goals and actively create opportunities. To be determined is to believe in yourself and your basic human rights. You are worthy of achieving happiness. You act on this internal self-esteem. Despite the risks, obstacles, and limited resources, determined individuals accept that if they want something, they have to work hard for it! At times, others may appear to have more advantages or unlimited resources than you, but your belief in the possibility of getting (or becoming) what you want is a valuable force in overcoming such real and perceived obstacles.

The Three D's of Determination

Destiny

Charismatic individuals own their decisions, accept their failures, and refrain from blaming others or list reasons why something didn't go their way. If you have given up on getting what you want or deserve, settle for less, or take the easy way out, then you are admitting defeat – the opposite of determination. You decide where you want to go and take responsibility for what it takes to get there, as opposed to letting other conditions or people dictate that for you.

Diligence

A stick-to-it approach to life and leadership is called *diligence*. When you least feel like doing a particular task, sometimes the only thing that sustains you is the heartfelt, "don't give up!" emotion. Anyone who has ever accomplished anything has done so with diligence. Many of my associates in higher education who earned their doctoral degrees often comment that doing so tested their diligence more than anything else! William Feather said, "Success seems to be largely a matter of hanging on after others have let go."

Decisiveness

If you've ever looked at someone and said, "Make a decision already!" you understand the frustration of watching others do nothing because they have too many choices. Individuals with Zing! make decisions. They commit to something. If it doesn't work out you will have to make adjustments, but at least you are moving. Any good sailor knows to keep trimming his/her sails along the way because being in motion is better than stalling out.

Be willing to risk doing something wrong over doing nothing at all. The next time you are indecisive ask, "What's the worst thing that could happen?"

In *The Contrarian's Guide to Leadership*, Steven B. Samples offers the point of view of doing nothing as the possible right course of action. The contrarian leader's approach to decision-making is to: "Never make a decision yourself that can reasonably be delegated to a lieutenant and never make a decision today than can reasonably be put off until tomorrow." In other words, carefully consider not acting as an option as opposed to not acting out of fear or procrastination.

In the classic bestseller *Awaken The Giant Within*, motivational icon Anthony Robbins tells a story of his early desire to be a public speaker. Making the point about determination, he remembers hearing many bad speakers who, despite their lack of skill, were still getting hired. He realized that if he was any good, he could become quite successful. He also realized that the best way to become a great speaker was to practice. To this end, he set a goal of speaking once a month. Then, he deduced that if he spoke once a week, by the end of the year he would have had 52 opportunities to practice, instead of only 12 opportunities. This still wasn't enough. So, he re-thought his approach and decided to speak twice a week, making almost 104 opportunities to improve his skills and build exposure. Anthony Robbins became one of the country's top speakers in a relatively short amount of time because he had a clear vision, good decision-making skills, and diligence.

Final Words on Vocabulary

Determination requires you to ask for what you want with clear, distinctive language while refusing to apologize for wanting people to follow your lead or assist you. To be determined is to believe in your capabilities and potential. Statements like, "I need you to…" or "It is important that you…" are more effective than, "If it's not too much of an inconvenience…" or "I know this may be an imposition, but…" Statements like "Here's what I'm going to do…" versus "Someday, I'd like to…" suggests your affirmative direction. Saying, "I will do what it takes to…" versus "I'll see where the chips may fall…" suggests that you control your destiny. To have Zing! you will need to practice being decisive and determined in your speech. Remember to respect others' basic human rights, however, including their right to say, "No" to you.

INFLUENCE 13 INITIATIVES

- Want something.
- Have a sense of your future or a vision.
- When discouraged ask, "What's the worst thing that can happen?"
- Decide to change something.
- Be clear in your language.
- Work around (or ignore, if needed) those who create obstacles.
- Reward yourself for all accomplishments – small or large.
- Examine your priorities and eliminate time spent on things that don't matter.
- Simplify and focus.
- Replace the words "I don't know what to do," with "I'm going to give it a try."
- Remember that you do not have to ask for permission to be happy.

Chapter 22

INSIGHT FOURTEEN
The Art of Interpersonal Communication

"Person to person. Touch to touch. Face to face.
Hand to hand. Heart to heart. Soul to soul. Eye to eye.
These are the true mediums of human communication.
Everything else is just a technological accomplishment –
an interfacing of our intellects."
- Nancy Hunter Denney

I can't dance. Despite this fact, when Al Green starts to sing I am compelled to move. Much to my daughter's embarrassment, I can't help myself because I love to dance. My husband can't dance either. He hides this reality by dancing what he calls the "yard-and-home-maintenance" dances which require minimal stepping and standing still. Maybe you've seen these special forms of expression: the lawn mower, hedge clipper, paintbrush, or water sprinkler! I completely understand why people tape over their wedding videos. Walk with me and talk with me; won't you please invite me to dance?

What does your dancing style say about you? You are never *not* communicating something! Your ability to express your ideas, articulate your goals, ask for what you want, and challenge others' assumptions requires you to carry your communication skills with you at all times. Effective communication is essential for building healthy relationships, challenging others' development, protecting basic human rights, enacting change, relating on higher levels, getting what you want, and giving others what they need. A high ZQ requires high skills of communication which is made possible by greater awareness, replacing ineffective skills with more useful ones, and practice. It is also helpful to understand the process.

There are two kinds of communication; the first is composed of the three basic elements of communication: sender, receiver, and message. *One-way communication* occurs when one person sends a message to a receiver in the absence of feedback like sending an email, giving a lecture, posting a sign, and writing an article. You never really know if what you sent was received as intended resulting in misinterpretation and misunderstanding. This form of communication is impersonal and is equitable to mass-marketing where "one size fits all."

When you add a feedback loop, you provide the receiver to respond to your message thus giving you the opportunity to check for their comprehension, as is the case with personal conversations, instant messaging, and phone conversations. *Two-way communication* works best when you are face to face with someone, because you have more to "read" and will lead to more accurate exchanges. The opportunity for active exchanges and a mechanism for offering and receiving feedback must be present for this form of communication, as in a phone call. Email is not two-way communication.

The significance of recognizing the type of communication to use helps you to focus your energies of influence where they are best served. Ask, "Should this be a phone call, email, letter or face to face encounter?" before you shoot off an email, or leave a nasty gram! Make the medium and message match. One-way communication, for example, is most appropriate when the receiver's opinion or response is not needed or requested. Your goal is to praise, honor, celebrate, recognize, lecture, or inform. You don't jeopardized how others might feel because the outcome of your communication won't be affected. However, when you want to respect someone's opinion, give them an opportunity to defend themselves, collect information about their feelings, show empathy towards potential concerns they might raise, or enter into a helping exchange, you have no choice but to use two-way communication.

Considerations for Effective Exchanges

There's no doubt you can learn to have Zing! because all of the necessary Insights are learnable skills. Practice them. If it scares you to meet new people or be in networking situations, prepare a strategy for "working the room" before you step foot in the room. Susan Roane in *How to Work a Room* notes, "You can learn to overcome many of the roadblocks or obstacles preventing you from talking to strangers." Like any skill, the more you practice, the more you improve.

Unlearn skills contrary to your charismatic mission and replace them with more useful ones. If you are overly aggressive, for instance, you can learn to tone down your forcefulness by consciously considering before you speak how to achieve your goals without coming on too strong. One approach is to listen for common ground and let the other person lead the conversation. Say little, but listen a lot. Instead of going for the long pass down the field, take it five yards at a time.

The second consideration for effective communication is to worry less about others' skills and more about your own skills. Focus on your skill building. You do this by taking responsibility for making strangers feel comfortable in your presence by walking up to them, extending your hand and saying, "I've never been comfortable in certain social settings, but this one looks like fun." Humor is always a nice way to break the ice, as is starting a conversation around a mutually accessible topic. Try to avoid the weather – that's been over done! Attend to your body posturing, spatial proximity and non-verbal gestures like crossing your arms because that is perceived as distancing not welcoming. To get a better idea of how effective others perceive your skills, take the exploration, The Art of Communication found in Appendix C.

Lastly, know there are many different types of communication skills. Just because you are proficient at one or two doesn't mean you are proficient at all of them. For instance, speakers who write are often accused (by editors) of writing like we speak! We are good at oral communication, but not necessarily at expressing ourselves on paper. Knowing this information is helpful because it encourages speakers who write to hire good editors. There are many skills of communication. Which do you do best: rhetoric, public speaking, written expression, mediation, paraphrasing, counseling, listening, assertiveness, confrontation, documentation and research, conflict resolution and interpersonal?

Three Valuable Skills

Managing Noise

You can never control 100% of the potential distractions affecting your ability to communicate because there are numerous variables potentially altering the meaning of your message or ability to communicate, referred to as noise. Frequently, such distractions are in the receiver's head! However, you can greatly increase your odds of effective communication by quickly asking, "What is going to interfere with my communication?" There are different kinds of "noises" to be listening for in your communications: Psychological noise includes mind distractions like length of attention spans, impressions, preconceived ideas, prejudices, insecurity and lack of confidence; Physical noise includes visual items (or people) blocking the receiver's vision or attention and make paying attention difficult; Hunger or pain noise is an internal physical noise taking the focus off of you; Stress noise is a combination of what's going on in someone's head and the physical reaction it is causing from nervous stomach to shaking; and Environmental noise includes not only visual distractions, but sounds, temperature, time of day, room arrangement and any other external potential interference caused by the elements around you.

Assertiveness

We have talked about the confidence and high self-esteem associated with influence and suggested Zing! personalities come in all shapes and sizes – one size doesn't fit all. You will need to assert yourself to make things happen, whether you are shy, quiet or overly pushy. Assertiveness is a style of communication designed to protect your basic human rights without violating another's basic human rights. It involves saying what you want without apologizing, clarifying your intentions, and being direct in your communications. It is how you appropriately show concern, disapproval and disagreement.

Confrontation

Bringing something to someone's attention to positively affect change is confrontation. It is not bad, violent or wrong to confront someone, yet is a skill many dislike because they believe it to originate out of conflict. Confrontation is rooted in love. For example, you may be uncomfortable giving someone an inadequate job performance, have a concern over a particularly harmful behavior of a friend, or need for a colleague to "step up to the plate" and work more collaboratively with you. These are admirable goals of your influence, and will require the skill of confrontation. To not say something and let inappropriate behavior continue is an Individual Detractor. More importantly, you allow people who are ignorant, unethical, and harming others to continue such behavior. Confront because you care.

INFLUENCE **14** INITIATIVES

- Practice improving your communication skills with strangers.

- Manage your emotions during conversations.

- Seek higher levels of reasoning as opposed to a higher volume.

- Never raise your voice to someone unless safety is a concern.

- Let silence happen.

- Use phrases like "Let me be clear..." to signal your request.

- Rearrange your space so people find you approachable.

- When confronting someone, don't sit behind an object.

- Practice smiling at strangers.

- Speak up for those who don't speak up for themselves.

Chapter 23

INSIGHT FIFTEEN
The Attraction of Listening

"About communication: I know you believe you understandwhat you think I said. But, I'm not sure you realize that what you heard is not what I meant."
- Andy Warhol

The hardest aspect of listening is that you have to stop talking. That's right. You must close your mouth. You must stand or sit without saying a word. Sounds rather simple, doesn't it? It would be if during the process of listening, you not only heard what is being said, but what isn't being said! Effective listening is essential to maximizing your Zing! because it allows your friends, significant others, family members, co-workers, employees and complete strangers, to connect with you at an interpersonal level. When you actively listen, you make a large non-verbal statement about how important other people are to you.

People are very perceptive. To actually listen after you ask, "How are you today?" speaks volumes, as does following a question with silence in order to give the other person time to formulate his/her thoughts. To not complete others' sentences, cut people off, or look over someone's shoulder when they are speaking to you represent the greatest compliments (or signs of respect or praise) you can give another human being. As suggested in the last chapter, the primary goal of communication is enhanced understanding. You can't achieve this goal if you don't accurately hear what is being said. Effective listeners understand what listening is not: an opportunity to think of what to say next!

Despite the fact you've been doing it all your life, you can improve your ability to listen because active listening is a learnable skill characterized by the ability to receive or understand the meaning, content and emotion of a communication as it was intended by the sender(s). To listen with accuracy requires the ability to be open, free from judgment, outwardly receptive, and actively engaged or attentive to others' thoughts as they communicate them. You need to hear what they are saying, not what you want to hear. This becomes easier the more you get to know someone. However, when you are unfamiliar with someone's interpersonal style and intentions, you must rely on other skills like paraphrasing.

The art of *paraphrasing* is the art of playing back what you just heard someone to say to you in your own words. You can respond to someone's comment with the prefix, "I hear you saying..." followed by a brief summary of the content of their remarks. Or you can say, "Sounds to me as if..." followed by your take of their remarks. A conversation is like a ping-pong match. You want to continually give back what you were just given. In most cases, the other person will let you know if you didn't understand their intention or the information they shared.

Visual Cues for Effective Listening

I have identified six significant "targets" or cues for effective listening. When you actively respond to these in every conversation you have, you greatly increase the odds you will eventually hit your mark and mutually enhance your understanding.

Body Language

Abraham Lincoln once said, "What you do speaks so loud, I cannot hear what you say." He was aware of the enormous power of non-verbal communication. Words can be manipulated much easier than body language. Research on communication varies in the actual percentage assigned to the significance of body language, from 60% to over 90%. You listen more to someone's actions, positions, and eye-contact than you do to their words. When in a conversation, pay attention to the possible messages being sent through body language as suggested below.

Messages of Meaning

Crossed arms = desire to "protect" yourself, blocking your presence, emotional distance

Hands on hips = pride, honor, sense of security, desire to appear firm or unyielding

Standing on one foot = insecurity, insincerity of message, uncertainty, fear, intimidation

Crossing legs while standing = same as standing on one foot, uncomfortable

Pointing = sense of superiority, aggressiveness, "fight-or-flight" attitude

Touching someone's arm = desire to get closer, warmth, interest in deeper relationship, fondness

Hands in hair = flirtatious, desire to be more casual or intimate

Shoulders raised = defensive, stiff or rigid, uncomfortable, unsure of self

Leaning against something = unsure of position, casual attitude

Walking slowly = weighed down, burdened, unhappy, hopeless

Walking quickly = free, nervous, happy, determined, angry

Smiling = comfortable, interested in establishing a relationship

Tight face = angry, tense, stressed, distant

Eye-contact = honesty, emotion, avoidance, or engagement

Content
　　The second target to set your eyes on is the actual content of the communication or words being spoken. For example, is the sender making an effort to impress you with his/her vocabulary? Is he/she refraining from using profanity? Both actions communicate a desire to look favorable. Conversely, be aware when a receiver responds with the use of slang or inside jokes. This may be a sign that they are not letting you into their club! In reality, they are putting you in your place.

Emotion
　　No matter how skilled you are at interpersonal communication, emotion is often difficult to read. You have to respond to the emotion of a comment before you respond to the content. When both emotion and content are congruent, you

are most likely getting accurate information. However, if you observe "nervous energy" when someone is talking to you, don't ignore it. Ask yourself, "Why is this person nervous? Should I trust the information? What can I do to address the source of his/her anxiety?" As previously noted, Zing! requires honesty. The honesty of your communication lives in the emotion of a statement rather than in the words.

Tone

Tone is the inflection communicated in the message. Tone involves rate of response, the sound (or pitch) of the voice, and/ or emphasis on certain words. A fast rate can indicate panic, anxiety, or excitement, whereas a slow rate can indicate sadness, shock, or confusion. A high-pitched voice usually coincides with the emotions of a fast rate of speech and a low-pitched voice with slow rate of speech. Emphasis on certain words can indicate sarcasm, anger, or even humor. Undoubtedly, tone is tricky to "hear," so you must take into account as many targets as you can grasp at one time.

Gender and Cultural Difference

The role of gender and cultural differences in effective listening deserve an entire chapter. Don't underestimate their significance! Research conducted by communication expert and author Dr. Deborah Tannen in *The Argument Culture* concludes there are gender differences in ways of speaking between men and women. She concluded, for example, men believe women nod to show agreement, whereas women nod to show they are listening! So, if I am in a conversation with a man and I am nodding to let him know I am trying to look attentive, he is really thinking how cool it is that I am agreeing with his every word! He sees me smiling which reinforces his assumption. I encourage you to read about gender issues in communication.

Similarly, understanding cultural differences in communication styles can greatly affect your ability to hear what is truly being said. The Hispanic culture is dynamic, vivacious and expressive. Loud does not mean rude. Talking over one another also is not considered rude. Yelling or arguing isn't interpreted as violent or uncivil. Once the argument has ended, no grudges are held. It's over. In other cultures, this would not be the case.

Eye-Contact

When you look into someone's eyes, you can see sadness, joy, commitment, intensity, wisdom, humor, loneliness, happiness, longing, desire and much more. To be an effective listener requires looking directly from your eyes into someone else's. This is often threatening because truth is found in the eyes. Did you know looking at the frequency someone blinks in your conversations can indicated how honest they are being with you? Recent research on the predictive value of rate of blinking and dishonesty in message found a positive correlation! Specifically, blinking rate increases when someone is being dishonest.

Not proved scientifically, but certainly is true in my experience, is another way of determining if someone is being truthful with you shared by a former colleague who handled judicial affairs at a university. She said, "If you want to know if someone just told you the truth, discuss the issue at hand: if they are skilled liars, they will maintain eye-contact with you. Then, change the topic. If they immediately look away from you, they were lying." She further explained in her experience, individuals can concentrate on maintaining eye-contact as long as they need to support their deceit. When they think they no longer need to keep up the front, their sub-conscious reacts by forcing their eyes to look away out of shame. Gotcha!

INFLUENCE 15 INITIATIVES

- Control for potential distractions.

- Interpret messages being spoken through the content, body language, and tone of speaker.

- Hold important conversations when you are most attentive.

- Observe people in conversations.

- Experiment with nodding.

- Sit in the front row of class or closest to the person speaking.

- If you have language barriers, acknowledge them.

- When speaking to someone significantly taller or shorter, be seated.

- Use the word but cautiously – it usually negates anything spoken before it.

- Lean forward or inward when you want a conversation to continue.

- When you are too personally distracted to listen effectively, honor the other person by saying: "I'm very interested in hearing your comments; however, I cannot give you my full attention right now. Can we reschedule?" This is far better than appearing uninterested.

Chapter 24

INSIGHT SIXTEEN
The Pull of the Podium

"Before I start speaking, I have something important to say."
— Yogi Berra

Imagine the pomp and circumstance of one of the most memorable commencement exercises in history. The scene is Oxford University. Under a nearby tent, a brass quartet plays Voltaire. To your right, someone fusses with his camera and behind you, a little girl plays with her long braid as her grandmother leans over and whispers, "Settle down." Something great is about to happen. The graduates enter in a formal march. However, all eyes are fixed on the party leading the processional. After a series of traditional remarks, the audience leans forward in anticipation for the commencement speaker. Even the graduates appear focused on something other than their own success. On cue, Winston Churchill stands and walks with purpose to the podium and says, "Never, never, never give up." Then, sits back down to take the record for the shortest — and most famous — commencement speech ever delivered. It is one of the most famous speeches ever delivered!

What do Ronald Reagan, Elizabeth Dole, John F. Kennedy, Jr., Gloria Steinem, Reverend Billy Graham, and Susan B. Anthony have in common? All were known for their exceptional oratory skills. Their success and achievements were due in large part to their ability to persuade their audiences to act. They just seemed to have "it." In more recent years, excellence at the podium is thankfully returning. Despite the barrage of comedy sketches depicting a rather recent President's inadequacies as a public speaker, those recently seeking the Office of President were rather accomplished in their speaking skills. This is one reason why record number of voters tuned in, or turned up, to hear well delivered, clearly articulated speeches by a host of candidates. Not only were they well written they were also well delivered.

You will know a great speaker when you hear one. By observing great speakers, you improve your ability to identify the consistent traits that make them great. While driving, I enjoy listening to audiotapes of great speakers. This practice teaches me to listen far beyond the content or words and attend to the manner of delivery, style, use of silence, and passion in their voices. Dr. Martin Luther King, Jr. not only mastered all of these components, but possessed an incredible ability to use rhetoric to literally change the world. Word combinations like "valley of despair" or "divine dissatisfaction" create a picture in your mind and inspire emotion in your soul.

The more you speak, the more you improve your speaking skills. Have you ever listened to someone speak and became nervous for them? Practice is the one thing that will improve your speaking ability. You can read all the books you want, hire a coach, but the only true way to get better at speaking in front of others is to actually speak in front of others! If you do get a speaking coach, be aware they are being compensated to get your results. They know where you started so come from a different perspective than someone hearing you for the first time. Risk the truth of asking someone for their opinion of your efforts – or resort to how most professional speakers get feedback about a speech: hang out in the bathroom behind a stall with your feet up!

It's not easy to speak when the stakes are high. In fact, I make up words all the time while speaking publicly, but keep on going. When you are the president, the CEO of a company, the "face" of an organization, or running for political office, there is an expectation of podium performance. It comes with the job. Your ability to Zing! at the podium is a requirement for your life and leadership.

The Benefits of Putting Yourself Out There

The true pull of the podium is that it gives you an opportunity to honor those you are blessed to serve by informing them, recognizing their talents, inspiring them to greater achievements, bringing them to a shared mission, and asking them to consider different points of view. Thousands of professional speakers, politicians, and celebrities live in America today. But where are the visionary voices? The answer is closer than you think. Survey after survey I conduct with my audiences reveals they are turning to people in their more immediate environments, schools, organizations, jobs, communities, and local governments for lessons on life and leadership. They are listening to and seeking visionary thinkers, articulate philanthropists and people willing to take a stand. If you are in their presence, you have that potential! Speak up and often!

Benefits of Enhanced Public Speaking Skills

You will become extremely perceptive of your audience's non-verbal communication. If you fail to read your audience correctly, you might continue to talk after your allocated time has run out and miss people looking at their watches, fixing their coats, rocking in their seats and looking annoyed that their time hasn't been respected. My first lesson on public speaking is: "Never, never, never speak longer than assigned!"

You will learn instinctively what methods, rhetoric, and style are most effective at evoking emotion in others. All oratory is persuasive. If you can't inspire your audience to listen and act, you are just a talking head. According to Dr. Will Keim, author of *The Keys to Success in College and Life,* "The art of public speaking demands precision in detail, persuasion in appeal and passion in delivery."

You have an opportunity to think about and organize your thoughts prior to speaking. The organization of a speech includes being concise, direct, captivating, and entertaining, while making no more than five major points.

The chance to experiment with a more entertaining or passionate you. Many speaking programs will teach you to stay at the podium. As I noted earlier, I'm five feet tall – or short. I am not comfortable when talking from a structure that is taller than I am! It is an individual detractor. By using humor and experimenting with various mediums and use of stage space, you develop your personal style.

You build a positive reputation by doing something most people are afraid to try. According to many sources, public speaking is the number one fear (number two being death) of people. Have the courage to give your ideas a forum of expression and the light shines directly on your life and leadership for all to see. This is a good thing.

You become more confident in your abilities. Improvement comes with effort – even if it doesn't go well the first few times. Learn from what works and what needs work.

You keep your job or get a job. Public speaking plays a more significant role in our life's job description than most are willing to accept. Don't let your fear or past performances stop you from stepping up to the plate, running for town office, or moving up the corporate ladder. Effective speaking requires risk-taking.

Exploration: Characteristics of Effective Speakers

Directions: Which of the following characteristics do you find appealing in the speakers you've heard? Pick someone you've heard recently, whether a teacher, professional speaker, pastor or anyone who spoke publicly and you found worthwhile. Think of at least four people. For each, check which traits they possessed. Consider the conditions under which they were delivering their remarks, your frame of mind and the challenges they had to overcome.

_____*Well-prepared*

_____*Humorous*

_____*Stick to the allocated time frame*

_____*Present original thoughts*

_____*Don't make excuses for being "bad"*

_____*Voices change in volume, tone and rate*

_____*Tell personal stories*

_____*Comfortable with silence*

_____*Play on different emotions*

_____*Refrain from condescending attitude*

_____*Appearances are appropriate for setting*

_____*Enjoy being on stage*

_____*Refrain from criticizing their audience or offending even one person*

_____*Respectful*

_____*Avoid holding a glass of water and/;or shaking it*

_____*Thank sponsors or show appreciation to their audience*

_____*Don't read a speech*

_____*Maintain eye-contact with the audience*

_____*Interact with audience members prior to the program*

_____*Smile*

An exceptional presentation can sometimes save a poorly-written speech. Audience members are so entertained they overlook a lack of substance in favor of being amused. Why not have both; great delivery and a great speech? To begin working on improving your speaking skill set, review the exploration, Public Speaking Homework found in Appendix D. This exploration evaluates the frequency of effective traits, many of which are listed below. The more consistently you incorporate the following characteristics of effective speakers and speeches into your effort, the higher your ZQ.

- *Hook the audience in the first few seconds*
- *Cover five or less main points*
- *Back up points with relevant stories, examples, or statistics*
- *Sequence points so they flow logically*
- *Inspire a variety of emotions*
- *Explain the "contextual relevancy" of the topic to audience*
- *Close with a connected hook used to open the speech*
- *Include follow-up by referring a web-site*
- *Leave the audience wanting more*
- *Provide accurate references to quoted material*
- *Reiterate the five or less major points*
- *Topic is appropriate to the setting*
- *Use a variety of mediums (between two to five) to make a point*

INFLUENCE 16 INITIATIVES

- Know your audience: male/female ratio, level of education, expectations, general professional experience, and motivation for attending the program.
- Adjust your program to meet the needs of the environment and audience.
- Give people a chance to warm up to you.
- Progress from non-threatening material to more challenging topics.
- Keep your language and thoughts one step (not ten) above your audience.
- Don't make people feel stupid in your attempt to sound smart.
- Draw from the audience's experiences whenever possible.
- Write your comments in outline form and staple the outline together.
- Practice from your outline until it fits on a napkin.
- Count on your technology to fail.
- When using PowerPoint, never look directly at the presentation screen.
- Never use PowerPoint – be the performance!
- If you do need PowerPoint get a remote clicker.
- Never criticize a response or answer from an audience member.
- Challenge inappropriate remarks.
- Compliment your audience whenever possible.
- Avoid profanity at all costs.
- Respect your audience.
- Make your points with different mediums.
- Remember: No one knows what your outline contained but you!

Chapter 25

INSIGHT SEVENTEEN
The Building of Relationships

*"The more people you know and who know you in a
positive way, themore likely it is that you will know
the right person at the right time forthe right reason
to take advantage of the right opportunity."*
- Brian Tracy

As a child, I identified with Casper the Friendly Ghost. I thought it would be rather exciting to float through walls, listen in on conversations and fly above houses. I could go wherever I wanted, whenever I wanted. Being invisible seemed appealing. But by the time I hit the sixth grade, it didn't seem like so much fun anymore. In fact, to be unnoticed was devastating. When did you first realize that you wanted to be noticed?

Putting them in a league of their own, individuals with Zing! notice everyone regardless of position, status, size, appearance, duty, age, race, gender, ability to advance their career or how fast they are moving. When you have Zing! you need to make people feel like they matter. You prefer to have exchanges with others go beyond dismissive greetings to more genuine interactions. Your goal is to leave people feeling like human beings and more worthy in your presence, regardless of their position – or your position.

Early in my professional career, I didn't get it. One of the greatest Individual Detractors in my charismatic portfolio was the manner in which I treated my secretary. Although she worked every day to ensure that my work was done, I never really noticed her or made her feel as important as I could. Sometimes I would say, "Good morning!" and in the same breath, ask, "Would you do this for me, please?" I focused on my needs, instead of her needs. I had no Zing! whatsoever. My ignorance of Dale Carnegie's lessons on "how to win friends and influence others" also included the non-charismatic practice of calling someone to obtain information and neglecting to ask about their life or make them feel valued before I politely asked for what I needed. I forgot what it felt like to be Casper – to be invisible.

Questions of Life and Leadership:

> *Do you make people feel invisible by accident or design?*
> *Do you notice, acknowledge, and treat the person who crosses your children at the crosswalk every day the same way you notice, acknowledge, and treat the school's principal?*
> *Does the person who empties your trash can at the office get the same respect and acknowledgement as the person who sits across from you at your staff meeting?*

Simply knowing someone's name is not the same as knowing them. My mother used to say, "To have a good friend, you must be a good friend." Your ability to walk into a room of 100 people and make each one feel as if they are the most important person is indicative of the value you place on building relationships. As we build upon previous chapters, it makes sense to examine the kind of relationship you have with yourself; specifically, do you like you?

Questions of Your Relationship with You:

> *If you didn't have to, would you hang out with you?*
> *Would you want to be supervised by you?*
> *Would you want to share an office with you?*
> *Would you want to serve on a committee with you?*
> *Would you marry you?*

Knowing yourself is an important step in establishing meaningful relationships. The truth revealed in the quip by Groucho Marx suggests the value in being wholly aware of what you bring to relationships. Marx said, "I would never join a club that would have me as a member." Taking a slightly different approach, Steven Covey writes in one of the best resources on personal development ever written, *The Seven Habits of Highly Successful People*, "The key to valuing [the mental, emotional, and psychological difference between people] is to realize that all people see the world, not as it is, but as they are." Therefore, to increase the quality of your relationships, you need to increase the quality you bring to your relationships! Consider the following factors that determine others' willingness to associate with you.

Characteristics of Zing! Connectors
Open Mindedness

Are you open to your co-workers' ideas, thoughts, and emotions, or do you shut them off and out? I recall having someone say to me once, "I don't want to talk about that; let's talk about what I want to talk about." Thinking he was joking, I laughed. Unfortunately, as I later learned, this high ranking self-proclaimed charismatic leader apparently said this in many of his conversations. His unwillingness to be open to other topics was a significant Individual Detractor. Be open to not only a diverse topic of conversation, but all of the other differences people can bring to a relationship like travel experiences, cultural upbringing, family, gender interests, educational pursuits and so on.

Trustworthy

Do you gossip? If you speak negatively of others, you tell the person with whom you are currently speaking that you can't be trusted to not speak negatively of him/her. Relationships require what I call the "comfort of connection." In the Conger, Kanungo and Menon study of follower effects (1998), "trust in a leader" was one of the variables linked to charismatic leadership.[1] They concluded, "The charismatic leader also builds follower trust through a demonstrated concern for follower needs, personal sacrifices, and unconventional expertise. . . They transform their concern for followers' needs into a total dedication and commitment to a common cause they share, and they express these qualities in a disinterested and selfless manner."

Lack Self-Importance or Ego

To build relationships, check your ego at the door. Replace it with humility. Let your talents speak for themselves. Remember the adage: If you have to tell someone just how good you are, you're not all that good!

Full Engagement

When in the presence of others, it matters whether you are happy to be there. You can demonstrate this by adding to the conversation, acknowledging their presence, and non-verbal language. Have you ever watched some men shop with their wives? These are not happy guys. I speak from experience. If you don't want to be somewhere, don't go! Despite your good intentions, you'll be a downer. Your lack of active engagement, smiling, participation, and slouching posture will pick up where your silence and grunts leave off.

Zing!

Follow Up

Oftentimes, the one determining factor between ongoing relationships and one-time encounters is your ability to follow up. Instead of saying, "We should get together," or "I hope to see you again," consider saying, "I've enjoyed meeting you; would you like to get together for coffee this week?" Always have a business card ready to give away. Even if you don't have an official title, you can have a business card that contains your contact information (specifically, your name, address, phone number, and email address). Keeping your cards in the box on your shelf isn't going to help a potential new contact remember you. Make a good impression from the start. I recommend using a leather business card case that allows you to keep your cards on one side and "incoming" cards on the other. This also protects your cards so they don't look like you've had them in your wallet for three years!

When with a group of people, following up takes more awareness to all members present; you can't ignore those you don't particularly like or connect with and make plans with those you do! That should be done in private so you don't hurt anyone's feelings. If people are standing together, don't invite one of them to join you for lunch and exclude all the other potential "Caspers" standing there. Treat everyone equally. If you see one, see them all!

Nurture

Lasting relationships get nurtured. They aren't left out there to fend for themselves. How can you make your relationships grow and how do you sustain them? For example, if you want to meet someone for coffee, don't ask the other person(s) to call you – you make the first move and honor them with a phone call! Elizabeth George, author of *Life Management for Busy Women* comments, "…it takes time, care, love, and money to nurture our relationships." She recommends, "purchasing little cards, small gifts, something that shouts out that person's name when we walk by, something [the other person] collects, uses, loves, enjoys, reads, and appreciates." Likewise, sending thank-you cards goes along way to express your desire to show someone your appreciation.

Time

Trust is the most developed stage of a relationship. When you aren't honest in your communications, or misread the commitment in a relationship, you interfere with another person's sense of comfort and his/her ability to be authentic. Because the process of relationship building is outward (not inward) and moves from what's on the surface (or small talk) to the inner realm of trust, give your first encounters time to turn into relationships – if you want them to.

Building Connections One Step at a Time

Understanding the process of establishing relationships will help you to connect and establish more meaningful relationships. You will also increase the probability of more authentic exchanges – whichever stage you are in. As suggested by the chart below, the important thing when building relationships is to be true to yourself, as well as, to the people you meet. If someone in your presence starts to go down a path that is morally inappropriate, you don't have to agree, laugh, or stay in that exchange. Don't lower your standards to gain a "friend" or win favor with someone. Instead, invite that person to raise his/her standards.

Denney Stages of Relationship Building

Stage of Relationship Building	Risk Level	Commitment Level	Nature of Conversations
1. Pseudo-Exchange (How can I make this person comfortable in my presence?)	None	Conditional	Superficial, introductions
2. Exploration (What do I need to know to determine if we can have a relationship?)	Low	Unsure	Approach more complex topics, remove barriers of communication, learning
3. Real Deal Decision (Is this a relationship I will take to a higher level?)	High	Move up or down	Important topics, look at values, vision of the future
4. Synergy (Am I a better person for knowing this person?)	Low	Something has clicked and you mutually benefit from the relationship	Most topics are acceptable, deeper level of conversation, real communication, varied emotions displayed
5. Trust (How can we become better people together?)	None	Unconditional	Sense of safety, motives pure and understood, failures are forgiven

The Difficulties or Complexities of Relationships

The reasons why someone might resist your overtures towards a relationship are complicated. Co-workers, for instance, have to work within an organizational structure and changing office dynamics. Supervisory roles represent potential struggles with authority, competition, and evaluation. When anyone has authority (real or perceived) over someone else, the playing field is not equal. When you are in a position of authority over someone else, you need to recognize the potential limits on your relationship and allow it to benefit the greater good. Deeper relationships are built when both parties are free to give and receive in the relationship.

In addition, you might not get to choose what your relationship becomes, or if you will interact again. Other factors, such as the setting, circumstance, or hidden agendas might mask the making of a true relationship. For example, during a recent conversation with a new friend, she confessed to resisting my initial overtures of friendship. Further conversation revealed that all of our meetings had been at social events where I tend to be very outgoing and she prefers to talk with people she knows well. To put Zing! in your relationships may require meeting someone on "neutral," but not beige ground.

Activities to Enhance Relationship Building

Network Effectively

The establishing of mutually beneficial relationships is called networking. Author of *The Networking Survival Guide* Diane Darling notes, "Networking is building relationships before you need them." The key to Zing! networking is to let others know how you can help them. In addition, you must continually create ways of maintaining communication with someone after you meet them. Whether this is a monthly cup of coffee, occasional phone call or card, if you want someone to remember you, you need to first remember them.

Shake Hands

There they are… at the end of your arms. Conveniently located and frequently ignored. One of the best ways to welcome or invite someone into your life is to extend your hand until it meets firmly with the other person's hand. If you have small hands, you need to squeeze a little tighter. If you have big hands, soften up on your grip. Maintain contact for a minimum of five seconds. To make your greetings warmer, consider holding your handshake even longer and placing your other hand over it.

Find an Inner Circle

Many high achieving individuals maintain an "inner circle" or small group of equally successful people to serve as spiritual guides, mentors, counselors, advisors and supporters. In many cases, their circle represents individuals who represent where they want to go (not where they've been). To think like a billionaire, for example, don't hang around with millionaires. Your inner circle should represent a diversity of support areas. Individuals to enrich the following areas of your life are suggested: financial, spiritual, emotional, grounding (or purpose), achievement (or career), and inspirational.

Remember Names

Ever forget someone's name as it is being introduced to you? Your name is like a key: offer it to others and invite them into your life and leadership. You want them to use it. When someone offers you his/her name, use it! Here are a few tips:

- *Repeat the name immediately upon hearing it so you learn to pronounce it correctly.*
- *Focus on the first name only.*
- *Don't go any further in your conversation until you can repeat the other person's name.*
- *Use the name again in the first fifteen words of your conversation.*

- *Ask for a business card to reinforce the spelling of their name.*
- *Repeat their name during the conversation at least three times.*
- *At the conclusion of your encounter, repeat their name again, so it's the last thing you say.*
- *Look down at their business card, after they leave.*

You can also make it easier for someone to remember your name by referring to yourself in the third person during your conversation. It sounds silly, but it is an effective way of putting your name out there again so the other person or party can remember it.

Small Talk

Remember! A conversation is a ping pong game. Keep serving up open ended questions like those beginning with how, why, what, and so on. Then, dig deeper. You can start with, "Tell me what brings you here?" or "How have you spent your time?" Small talk does not have to be meaningless. It's talk. Your goal, however, is not to do all the talking! Here are a few tips:

- *Pay a compliment early in the conversation.*
- *Smile often.*
- *Start sentences with "conversation triggers" such as: "Tell me about…" or "It's a beautiful day, what brings you here?" or "It's a pleasure to meet you. What are you hoping to do while you are here?"*
- *Avoid looking down when silence occurs – instead, look directly in the other person's eyes.*
- *If the other person is rather shy, help them out by saying, "I don't personally like these kinds of social events. Sometimes they make me feel uncomfortable. What kinds of events make you feel more relaxed?"*

- *Use the environment to your advantage. What do you see that you can reference as a common denominator? For example, "I'm impressed by our surroundings. How do you find the architecture?" or "What a beautiful room. I admit to entering a room and deciding exactly what wall I will be taking down! I'm a big fan of interior design and renovation. How about you?"*
- *Of course, remember to shake the hand of your small talk partner upon the greeting and after your conversation.*

Establishing relationships is like giving gifts. You can often tell from the wrapping that you're going to like what's inside. The Zing! relationship builder hands out gifts all day long knowing they might not get anything in return, yet hoping their gifts will be valued or "re-gifted."

Influence 17 Initiatives

- Remember! Every encounter is a chance to make someone's day.

- Be willing to create more meaningful exchanges and relationships.

- Verbally express how you value your relationships with others.

- Send a card or perform an act of kindness to someone you like.

- Leave every conversation with a word of praise for the other person.

- Find creative ways to keep the communication door open.

- Always carry business cards.

- At the end of a conversation, ask for someone else's business card.

- Stand when shaking someone's hand, maintain eye-contact and smile.

- Treat everyone with an equal amount of respect.

- Never make someone feel like Casper the Friendly Ghost.

- Make the effort to remember people's names.

- Associate with people who can help you achieve your dreams.

- Embrace diversity in your relationships.

- Remember people's birthdays and special occasions.

Chapter 26

INSIGHT EIGHTEEN
The Punch of Humor

*"Allowance is what you get for
saying you cleaned your room."*
- Kaitlin Elizabeth Denney

L augh and the whole world laughs with you. I don't know who made that statement but he/she understood the Zing! appeal of humor. Levity plays a wonderful role in drawing people together. I believe it's a universal language that transcends age, art, and cultural differences to bring joy and happiness to the world. If you don't believe that you are funny, you must at least believe you have the potential to bring joy and laughter to the world. You show others you care about them when you make them laugh. You make them feel worthy by creating playfulness, cheer, and happiness. Your light heartedness will be rewarded by their reactions. In fact, they might even return the favor! People will seek out those who lift them up, not bring them down. Funny people like to associate with people who make them laugh. Anyone who seeks enjoyment from life will quickly welcome a break from the stressors of life. The use of humor will draw people to you socially and professionally.

Have you ever started to laugh and can't stop? What begins as a chuckle turns into roll-on-the- floor laughter. Your stomach tightens, your eyes tear and you make snorting noises with your nose. As you start to collect yourself, you grip your belly and take deep breaths. Your laughing fit leaves you much more susceptible to laughing again. I have often watched very effective speakers get their audience laughing and keep them laughing. A magical exchange takes place in which the audience members transform from a "show me what you've got" mentality to active engagement. Zing! comes to life through laughter.

When you seek to be more humorous or laugh at yourself, you reveal humility. The ability to laugh at your own stupidity and silliness brings people towards you because they see you as human and wonderfully flawed. Levity can also break tension, reduce stress and you feel more relaxed. When appropriate, telling a joke or using humor to prevent tense exchanges or situations from escalating is masterful leadership. Laughter brings not only a psychological lift, but also a physiological lift. The chemicals released in your brain during laughter make you more relaxed, comfortable, and light-headed. When people are anxious, apprehensive, or nervous, use humor as a calming influence or distraction.

Humor is an effective way of reflecting your intelligence and wit. The most successful stand up comics are extremely bright individuals. They have a sharp wit and a keen perceptiveness to their surroundings. When you tell sophomoric jokes, you will be viewed as immature. When you use a more sophisticated wit, you will demonstrate maturity. Another benefit to the use of humor is it keeps you from going insane. Humor protects you, heals and as research indicates, will make you live longer! Many of the funny individuals in our lives have learned to be funny as a defense mechanism against the world. Instead of retreating into themselves to escape the pain of a difficult childhood, for example, they projected their energies outward. When you use humor to move your life forward, you attract (instead of push away) people, allowing for more interesting relationships and conversations. People will want to engage in conversations with you when you appear comfortable enough to share your humor with them.

What's So Funny?

It is theorized that laughter is like the brain "hiccupping." Your brain starts to follow a certain course of logic or reason or expectation and all of a sudden–hiccup–it registers something it didn't expect to get. Steve Allen has authored over forty-five books on humor, some are instructional; others are murder mysteries with creative and humorous twists. In his book *How to Be Funny: Discovering the Comic in You,* Allen notes how laughter is the result of: "the brain being forced to recognize an alternative explanation." You laugh because you expect one thing and get something else. Allen says, "...laughter is produced out of a sort of minor nervous explosion in the brain, a kind of short-circuit spark...the brain is momentarily startled... it's normal function interrupted. When you do the unexpected, you will make people laugh."

Humor relies on context and situation. Allen says, "The funniest things are not jokes we hear on the radio or on movie screens, but the real-life social faux pas, slips of the tongue, fumblings and bumblings that amused human beings for millions of years before anyone ever thought of being funny on a professional basis... Nothing is inherently amusing of itself; humor lies only in particular contextual relationships."[1]

He sites an example of when he played the straight-man to an unpredictable studio audience. This was a technique he mastered – live audience interaction. On one occasion, he asked a man: "What's your name?" In a reportedly calm voice, the man replied: "Boston, Massachusetts." At that very moment, he couldn't have said anything as funny as the audience member had just said in that situation. Allen notes the man's answer had "all the elements of true humor; it's ridiculous, absurd, entirely unpredictable, and comes as a lightning-quick surprise." Humor is a direct line to Zing!. You can become a funnier human being if you are willing to experiment with new behaviors. As a speaker, I've studied numerous methods of facilitating laughter.

How to Trigger Laughter in Others:

- Laugh.
- Make fun of yourself.
- Dance.
- Tell jokes that are appropriate, harmless, and clean.
- "Ad-lib" with strangers.
- Use witty word choice.
- Use satire to express different points of view, like the political satire of Jon Stewart.
- Try visual humor like a sketch or prop.
- Engage in or watching silliness or "child's play."
- Simple actions like the antics of Ellen DeGeneres or Lucille Ball.

Finding the Humor in a Room That Leaked

A few years ago, I found myself speaking at a "mandatory motivational" meeting of over six hundred students at a university in Missouri. It was pouring rain, end of the year exams were scheduled that same week, and students had to sign in to receive credit for attending my lecture. In other words, not a receptive audience.

Being the perceptive speaker that I am, I picked up on the many clues being left of the sentiment of my audience. First, upon entering, many students sat at a round table, faced their backs to the stage and took out their books. One group began sewing ribbons for their upcoming philanthropy. Another group actively sought out the tables furthest from the stage. Yet another group made non-discrete comments like, "This is going to suck."

I now had a choice. I could run and run fast. Or, I could play. Table by table, I stopped and made small talk with audience members trying intentionally to make them laugh. They did. At one table, I literally sat down and said, "Man, think it could rain a little more?" The gentlemen at the table said, "Hey, if it did those ceiling tiles over the stage would definitely crash down on the speaker. How cool!" I laughed and then turned towards the stage. Yes, the ceiling was leaking over the podium...

Instinctively, I turned back to my new best friends and said, "So, what's going on here tonight?" Leaning back in his chair and placing his feet on the table, one young man said, "Some speaker about car wrecks. We have to be here. It's mandatory." Further inquiry revealed that the last mandatory speaker came to fulfill a liability requirement for drunk driving prevention and showed a video with dead bodies. I got up, went to the stage, smiled at my companions and introduced myself. Clasping the hand-held microphone, I began to tell the story of my trip *from the East Coast to the university, describing in detail the three planes, decreasing in size as I came closer to Missouri, and the declining age of the pilots, noting the last pilots were wearing braces and carrying lunch boxes.*

My story continued with a lively description of the hour and a half drive to the hotel. I noted how disappointing it was in comparison to Boston driving, followed by a demonstration of Boston drivers: the changing of lanes, stopping in the center lane for no apparent reason, and cutting people off. My audience watched, attentive and amused. I even heard an occasional murmur of laughter.

Finally, after complaining about the rain, the tornado watch, and standing in my hotel room looking out at a potential natural disaster, I said, "It was at this point I really, really, really didn't want to come here tonight." And then, just as silence overtook the room, I quipped, "But, it was mandatory. I had to show up." The leadership speech went fine.

Deciding When to Play

In the above situation, I had to quickly decide whether to ignore the obvious, or use it to my advantage. The other option was to begin my remarks with, "I know you don't want to be here. But, I'm going to speak an hour of your lifetime away." When you make a conscious decision to play instead of fight or to look for the humor in a potentially humorless or challenging situation you can Zing! and people will respond positively to your attempts to make them happy.

Exploration: Playfulness is Serious Business

Directions. The following scenarios offer an opportunity for you to practice playful approaches to challenging situations. Your goal is to identify the response – or create one – that offers the benefits of playfulness, curiosity, and fun. Select the answer that best characterizes your understanding and application of playfulness.

Your friend informs you that he/she is considering running for the local school board. You...

— Send him/her an inspiring card.
— Send an email of congratulations.
— Wrap up an old pair of sneakers and send with a note, "Thought you might need these!"
— Take him/her out for lunch.
— _____

You have to work late, along with other colleagues, to meet a deadline. No one is particularly happy about the situation. You...

— Refrain from complaining.
— Go into your office and close the door to concentrate.
— Skip dinner.
— Tell everyone there will be a fifteen minute pizza party in your office at 8pm – they bring the drinks, you'll order the pizza.
— _____

You need to send your clients – or those you associate with professionally – some form of appreciation for their loyalty and business. You...

— Send them an email of appreciation.
— Send flowers and/or candy.
— Send two coffee mugs, gift certificate for coffee, and a note, "Next time, I'll come in person."
— Call them.
— _____

You are in a conversation with someone who is going on and on about absolutely nothing and you have to get going. You...
— Stand there nodding patiently.
— Ask the person if you can hug them.
— Look at your watch.
— Tell them you have to leave.
— _____

Someone has had good news – or reason to celebrate. You...
— Fill his/her office (or car) with balloons.
— Send a congratulations card.
— Take him/her out for lunch.
— Sing "Happy Birthday!" or an appropriate song.
— _____

Someone seated next to you on a plane takes off his/her shoes. Their feet stink. Your eyes are watering. You...
— Sit there and cry.
— Hit your call button.
— Smile and say, "OK, this means war. I'm going to take off my shoes, too!"
— Put a blanket over your head.
— _____

You are having a really bad day. You arrive home to a messy house. You...
— Blast your favorite CD pick up as you move to the music.
— Yell at your kids, cat, or dog.
— Throw everyone's clothes out the window (in honor of my mother's approach).
— Angrily pick up the mess.
— _____

You are delayed in an airport for five hours with strangers. You...
— Find the closest bar.
— Ask for the Customer Service phone number to complain.
— Play Hearts on your computer for five hours.
— Find the closest kid and see if he/she will play tic-tac-toe with you.

—

You have volunteered to substitute teach and walk into a room of less than motivated tenth graders just looking to make your day bad. You...
— Challenge them to a game of Simon Says.
— Tell them to sit down and shut up.
— Hide behind the desk and look busy.
— Pray.

—

Your dry cleaners don't have your clothes back when they said they would. You...
— Tell them you will never use their services again.
— Slam the door on your way out.
— Show them your receipt highlighting the due date.
— Smile and say, "How about a Big Mac and fries?"

—

Interpretation: You can change the outcome of most any situation by taking things less seriously. You will either make a situation better or worse by the type of energy you bring to it. Look for the humor, fun, and chance to play with people of all ages. The responses I intended to be playful in the above quiz include: 1.c 2. d 3. c. 4. b 5. a 6. c 7. a 8. d 9. a 10. d How did you do? If you chose the playful responses, you get the point. If not, it's time to put on a party hat and get silly!

Staying Within Good Taste

The tricky thing about humor, however, is to avoid going overboard to the point of poor taste or no taste. Experimenting with humor can be risky, especially if your humor is inappropriate despite what you think. Sarcasm is sometimes used to in an attempt to be funny, and can get you into trouble. Sarcasm is the attempt to be funny by being "subtly aggressive" at someone else's expense. It should only be used when directed at inanimate objects not people. When directed at a person or group, sarcasm is a form of aggression – not humor. It violates someone's basic human rights by tricking the other person, or group, into believing they aren't being picked on, attacked, or insulted. In reality, that's exactly what you are doing. It's usually a good idea to steer clear of sarcasm – most people don't care for it, and it matters what people think!

Tips for Offensive Free Speaking:

- Never under any circumstance use male or female bashing to make people laugh.
- Experiment with different jokes or personal stories before taking them public.
- Delivery and content is just as important as the content of a personal anecdote or joke.
- Physically "get into" your story or joke. If it involves someone walking, for instance, mimic walking as you paint the visual picture.
- Never make people laugh at the expense of someone other than yourself.
- If you are using an anecdote from another source, don't pass it off as yours. Properly reference someone else's creativity.
- Take the hint. If someone is kind enough to tell you "that wasn't funny," believe them.
- When in doubt, leave it out.

- Avoid crossing the line between "fabrication" and "exaggeration."
- Practice your jokes or monologues in front of other people before using them in high stakes situations.

INFLUENCE **18** INITIATIVES

- Believe you can learn to be funny.
- Buy a book by Steve Allen and Jon Stewart.
- Observe funny people.
- Go to a comedy club.
- Hang around funny people.
- Listen to comedy CDs or tapes.
- Observe the playfulness and silliness of children.
- Write jokes and test them on strangers.
- Look for humor every day.
- Ask people about their funniest moments.

Chapter 27

INSIGHT NINETEEN
The Appeal of Playfulness

"The child is in me still...and sometimes not so still."
- Fred Rogers

"It's a beautiful day in your neighborhood, won't you be my neighbor?" These words were the trademark of Mr. Fred Rogers. His red cardigan sweater symbolized a shift from the formal to the comfortable. It was his invitation to play. To not like Mr. Rogers wouldn't stop him from liking you. His living room became our living room. His purpose in life was to provide children with a source of entertainment founded in such values as love, compassion, education, and good spirited fun. To fulfill this purpose, Mr. Rogers was a creator, composer, puppeteer, and musician. He earned a graduate degree in child development and became an ordained Presbyterian minister. He also founded the non-profit organization Family Communications, Inc. to ensure his vision of children's television programming would endure.

Despite his numerous recognitions, including being inducted into the Television Hall of Fame, Mr. Roger's greatest legacy is the way he made children feel when they watched *Mister Rogers' Neighborhood* on PBS. This is where Mr. Rogers clearly loved to play. After his death in 2002, Mr. Rogers' wife compiled and published a wonderful collection of his favorite sayings and quotes. By reading *The World According to Mr. Rogers*, you begin to understand how he managed to positively influence generations of Americans. Mr. Rogers speaks to the seriousness of play when he said,

> *"Play does seem to open up another part of the mind that is always there, but that, since childhood, may have become closed off and hard to reach. When we treat children's play as seriously as it deserves, we are helping them feel the joy that's to be found in the creative spirit. We're helping ourselves stay in touch with that spirit, too. It's the things we play with and the people who help us play that make a great difference in our lives."* [1]

Defined as a sense of adventurousness or creative spirit, *playfulness* is identified in numerous sources as an appealing and overridingly consistent trait found in successful individuals and leaders. In *Geeks and Geezers*, Warren Bennis and Robert Thomas define the concept of playfulness as neoteny.[2] They discovered that every one of their "geezers" (leaders who were 25 years old between 1945–1954) had the "wonderful qualities associated with youth; curiosity, playfulness, eagerness, fearlessness, warmth, energy." These traits kept them hungry for knowledge and discovery. They also observed, "The capacity for uncontaminated wonder, ultimately, is what distinguishes the successful from the ordinary, the happily engaged players from whatever era from the chronically disappointed and malcontent."

Sounds Fishy

The *Fish Philosophy* was inspired by Dr. Lundins' youthful experiences as a camp counselor for children with Muscular Dystrophy, cancer, and other significant health conditions. It became known to the world in the bestselling book *Fish*, written Stephen C. Lundin, Ph.D., John Christensen, and Harry Paul. Although it took almost forty years before he was able to write the many life lessons he had learned about courage, determination, suffering, joy, life, and death, while at camp, Dr. Lundins' Zing! caused a worldwide attitude change – the catalyst was a local fish market.

While filming a documentary in Seattle, Dr. Lundin and his friend, a video photographer, went to a local fish market to buy fish. Customers flocked to this particular market in recognition of its cooperative, productive, and playful atmosphere. As he observed the silliness and spirit around him, Dr. Lundin was reminded of the same themes present during his earlier days at camp. The Fish Philosophy was born. The FISH approach to life recommends you do the following:

> *Play.*
> *Make their day.*
> *Be there.*
> *Choose your attitude.*

Dr. Lundin's early observation about human behavior stood the test of time: When you make something fun (even something as potentially disgusting or slimy as beheading fish) you will attract people to the activity, and this includes its purpose, planners and participants. Playfulness is an attitude as well as an activity. When you make play part of your character, you make a decision to view the world from the eyes of a child. Aldous Huxley said, "The secret of genius is the ability to carry the spirit of the child into old age, which means never losing your enthusiasm."

Characteristics of Playful People:

- *Laugh at their own silliness*
- *Create adventure*
- *Take the road less traveled*
- *Stop to smell the roses*
- *Fill their time with productive activities*
- *Make hobbies part of their every day*
- *Curious about how things work*
- *Ask "what if" questions*
- *Look for more than one answer*
- *Invite other people into their "sandbox"*
- *See colors as opposed to black and white (or beige)*
- *Kind hearted and warm*
- *Forgiving of failure – yours and theirs*
- *Intentionally and unintentionally make others laugh*
- *Hungry for knowledge*
- *Play games*
- *Possess positive energy*
- *Enjoy recreation, activity, and movement*

Life and Leadership through Playfulness

One of the most charismatic and influential individuals I know is a vice-president of student affairs at a major university in New York State by the name of Dr. Dennis Black. He has a national reputation for his work in legal affairs in higher education. Despite the seriousness of his subject area, Dr. Black embraces playfulness as a leadership tool and has the most Zing! of anyone I know. He uses it masterfully to put others at ease and relieve potentially stressful situations. When combined with his ability to see the bigger picture, Dr. Black inspires the best in others and can accomplish great things from raising two civic minded intelligent children, to being the chairperson of a national conference. He would be the first to comment, "I didn't do anything, the committee did!"

A Disney Don't

I first met Dr. Black while attending a conference in Orlando in 1997. It was hosted at one of the beautiful Disney properties and so I had decided to take my oldest child Jake with me. He was six years old. Before being able to take my son to Disney World, I had a speech to give. Little did I know, I was the one who was going to learn an important lesson about life and leadership: You can judge another's sense of playfulness and leadership potential by observing their interactions with children - especially your own.

While I was in the middle of giving a speech, Jake was ready to go to the park. At the least, he wanted to leave the banquet facility and let his wishes be known to the entire audience. Confusion erupted as the conference director carried my screaming son out of the room. Within seconds, I went from being in control to feeling an overwhelming concern for my son, combined with a big dose of embarrassment. I attempted to finish my speech.

Afterwards, as the room cleared, I looked for my child. A quick glance to my left did the trick. With big smiles on their faces, pant legs rolled up, and two ties around their heads (Ninja Turtle style) Jake and the afternoon keynote speaker, Dr. Black, skipped towards me. I developed instant admiration for Dr. Black's uncontaminated wonder and willingness to play with Jake.

Benefits of Playfulness

In the situation above, would you "jump in with both feet" or would you be too busy talking about the awkwardness of the situation? Would you have been offering to help or starting a "Worst Mother of the Year" petition on my behalf? Dr. Black's playful response spoke volumes about his approach to life and leadership. Playfulness is an effective tool in overriding competing forces to positively influence others, and in some cases like Mr. Rogers, Walt Disney, Charles Schultz, and Barney creator Sheryl Leach, turns into a lasting legacy literally changing generations of children. It is a contagious gift and comes with many perks: spreads joy to those around you; creates an environment of creativity and productivity; demonstrates a consistent desire to turn negatives into positives; makes you approachable; allows people to risk failure (and success) without penalty; makes you more imaginative and innovative; creates a sense of intrigue and curiosity about you; encourages others to be more playful and curious; and results in a higher quantity of ideas.

Learning How to Play Well with Others

Finding a playful way to accomplish your goals helps you to "go with the flow" instead of making those around you miserable. For example, if the projector breaks down in the middle of your presentation, is your ability to Zing! out the window as well? If you arrive at an organizational meeting to find twice as many people as expected with half as many chairs, are you stumped? Solve the problems in your life from the perspective of youthful vision or play. Look through the eyes of a child–play, create, and do the unexpected. Your other option is to see the glass as half empty and hate what's left in it! Play helps you find a water fountain. A playful approach to business has served Southwest Airlines well. While many airlines are going bankrupt, SWA earns profits using the mission statement, as reported in *A Whole New Mind* by Daniel Pink, "People rarely succeed at anything unless they are having fun doing it."

When you are playful, you can always answer the question, "So, what do you want to do?" Boredom is neither an option nor part of your repertoire. I believe: "Boredom is not a state of mind. Boredom is the state of not using your mind." When you are playful, you can also answer the question, "So, what do you think?" You are willing to contribute your ideas like you did when your kindergarten teacher asked a question and you had to hold your elbow to prevent your raised waving arm from falling off!

If you are a student, learn to play in class. Raise your hand. Ask questions. Sit on your knees and hold your elbow! If you are a parent, turn off your kid's TV and pick up a bat and ball. Go for a hike. Teach your kids how to bake a cake. Play a board game under a blanket in your living room. Remember, children will learn by watching your example. If you conduct the dullest staff meetings on the planet, start your next meeting with crayons and coloring books. If you change your approach from boring to Zing! you instantly change the environmental energy available to others from a negative to a positive!

INFLUENCE 19 INITIATIVES

- Hold a bubble gum blowing contest with yourself when no one is watching.

- Keep a coloring book and crayons in your desk.

- Color when you start to get too serious or stressed.

- Put colorful and cheerful reminders of your childhood in your environment.

- Dance. Skip. Jump.

- Play Simon Says at your next meeting.

- Read books on creativity.

- Read Doug Hall's Jump Start Your Brain.

- Before you freak out, ask, "Where is the potential for play in this situation?"

- Carry balloons in your pocket in case of emergencies.

- During your lunch hour, go to the playground and swing.

- Begin or revive a hobby.

- Doodle.

- Hand out lollypops.

- Wear a silly hat.

- Play a practical joke on someone.

- Hold chair races down the hallway.

- Try a game of musical chairs before your next committee meeting.

- While waiting in line at the grocery store play "I spy…" with the person behind you.

- Hang out with kids.

- Babysit your neighbor's kids.

- Schedule a "Game Night" with friends.

Chapter 28

INSIGHT TWENTY
The Gift of Self-Discipline

*"If we are to maintain confidence in ourselves,
we must be able to trust that we will do what
we say we are going to do."*
- Sue Patton Thoele

Tom Hanks' portrayal of Forrest Gump won him an Academy Award. His true reward was how his character inspired a nation. The writing was so masterful that many of the lines are now part of American culture, such as: "Stupid is as stupid does" or "Life is like a box of chocolates!" You can see this classic movie again and again, each time catching something you missed in earlier viewings. What fascinates me most about Forrest Gump is his self-discipline. He repeated specific behaviors despite the required physical, mental, and spiritual effort.

Whether your goal is to run from one coast to the other, lose weight, improve your GPA, lower your golf score, or increase your savings, some degree of regulation of your energies is required. Nothing is ever accomplished without a predetermined direction – or focus – of your efforts. This doesn't mean you must always know exactly how you want things to turn out; instead, you know that what you are doing is a step in the right direction.

The ability to control or direct your life for the sake of becoming a better person or achieving a desired outcome of self-improvement is called *self-discipline*. The word discipline can bring about a negative response. It comes from the word disciple meaning a learner who is in loving response to a respected teacher. With self-discipline you are both teacher and student. Self-discipline has the power to end up being the difference between those who want more for their life and leadership, and those who do what it actually takes to get more. It involves work, sacrifice and making tough decisions.

Influential and charismatic difference makers possess a high degree of this trait in order to make things happen. As you observe people with Zing! you come to admire their self-discipline because you know how hard it is to achieve on a daily basis. You are impressed by their perseverance, endurance, and determination. Many of us (myself included) could be doing much greater things and achieving at higher levels, but just aren't willing to work that hard or give up that much. Demonstrated in a variety of ways, self-discipline is best understood when contrasted to those with no or little self-discipline.

Exploration: The Look of Self-Discipline

Directions: Place a check mark next to the behavior in each row that best describes you a majority of the time?

List A: Disciplined Personality

_____ *Run every day*
_____ *Carry a bottle of water everywhere*
_____ *Snack on an apple*
_____ *Put yourself in "time out"*
_____ *Take a deep breath*
_____ *Maintain a healthy weight*
_____ *Eat healthy portions of food*
_____ *Breath clean air*
_____ *Manage time*
_____ *Drink alcohol in moderation*
_____ *Finish work on time*
_____ *Watch little to no TV*
_____ *Say, "I abstain from..."*

List B: Low Disciplined Personality

_____ *Drive to the corner store*
_____ *Over consume coffee*
_____ *Snack on candy bars*
_____ *Loss temper at children*
_____ *Slam doors*
_____ *Maintain too much weight*
_____ *Supersize all meals*
_____ *Smoke*
_____ *Always frazzled*
_____ *Binge drink*
_____ *Constantly submit late work*
_____ *Addicted to TV*
_____ *Say, "I just can't help myself..."*

Moving Forward with Self-Discipline

Is it possible you are anxiously waiting for life and leadership to happen to you, instead of working on the self-discipline necessary to achieve happiness? What conclusions do your colleagues, neighbors, employees and friends, draw about your potential to positively influence them based upon their perception of your discipline level? Although largely found on the surface, these characteristics will be perceived as indicators of your ability to self-regulate. They may have little to do with your actual competency or abilities, yet have everything to do with how you are seen by others.

Forrest Gump liked to run. He didn't always know to where he was running, just that he liked to run. In a classic scene, Forrest sets out running from the West Coast, unsure of his destination. Every time he gets to a new place, he decides to "keep on running." His direction is simply forward. Self-discipline allows you to move forward because you are letting go of self-doubt, insecurity, and the fears associated with change in favor of an internal drive to become someone different – someone better.

I am blessed to work with college students on a regular basis. From new-student orientations to commencement addresses, I observe their successes and failures. By the very act of going to college, they receive more choices and opportunities. Whether you are a returning or part-time student or just out of high school, your pursuit of a degree is a pursuit of self-discipline. This doesn't mean you know which degree you want! This doesn't mean you know what you will do with the degree once you get it! But you have put yourself in a position to achieve something – you'll figure out what that is when the time is right. The important thing is to want and be willing to expend lots of energy. Be hungry for a better you. Want a better world.

Components of Self-Discipline

Sacrifice

What are you prepared to give up? Are you willing to sacrifice time with your family to become the president of your company, or is that too high of a price? Do you have a bad habit like smoking or yelling at your children (or co-workers), but aren't ready to quit? Does the belief "you just don't have any more time" in your day override your desire to make a difference in your community? These are questions of sacrifice. Whether time, money, promotion, affiliation, friends, or favor, what are you willing to give up in pursuit of something greater?

Commitment

The ability to establish a sense of loyalty and trustworthiness through a repeated presence and exertion of energy is called commitment. To keep energized, use mental reminders like, "Am I in or am I out?" or "Jump on board or get off the boat!" In other words, commit fully or admit that the goal isn't really that important to you. Much like you can't be "slightly pregnant," you can't be half-hearted in your desire to make the world a better place. Help out by investing in what matters to you! Do what you can do, but do it fully. Lip service (i.e. "I want to help out, but I can't make it…") is not commitment.

Decision Making

Decision-making is the process of making choices based upon priorities. It's a process of getting rid of the junk in search of the jewels. Have you ever been paralyzed because you have so many options? Picture the process of decision making as a trip to the grocery store. Once you have put everything you want in your cart and make it to check out, you are informed of how much you have to spend! This forces you to put back what you really don't need or can't afford. You must prioritize what is most important to your life so you can avoid doing what doesn't serve that purpose. The key is to simplify and focus. Choose to work on only one or two self-improvement areas at a time. Give them your full attention. Apply a decision you are currently trying to make to the suggested process below:

The Decision Making Process

1. Write down all of your options (i.e. opportunities to make a difference).
2. Re-visit your purpose and philosophy of life statement.
3. Cross out those opportunities that don't fit or match up.
4. Examine the feasibility of what remains. Do you have the time, resources, and support, to pursue each option?
5. Identify the remaining items and determine what you need to sacrifice to make a full commitment to each option. Can you afford it?
6. Repeat steps two through five until you have only two options remaining.
7. Discussing these options with others. This practice gives you valuable feedback.
8. Although decision-making experts may use more professional terms... Go with your gut! Choose the one opportunity that feels right to you.

Structure

If you view self-discipline as a form of self-regulation, it makes sense to organize or make a routine of your behaviors. Individuals with Zing! structure their day. They reserve – or devote – certain parts of their day (and week) to the development or commitment of their wellness, spiritual health, family, community, or sense of play. Do you have a regular morning routine or are you all over the place looking for things? Are you able to find ten minutes before your feet hit the floor to pray or be appreciative? What activities can be put on a schedule to provide you with the emotional, psychological, and spiritual reserves you will need to make the world a better place one day at a time?.

Habits

Make your goals habits! When you make something a habit, you are more inclined to stick with it. Consider the difference between "going on a diet" or "being fit for life." The behaviors are identical; the mindset of a "dieter," however, is there is a beginning and an end. Fit individuals have integrated working out and eating well into their every day. They just don't eat Krispy Kreme donuts. One way to make something a habit is to associate the phrase, "That's just the way it is!" with a particular activity you want to either keep or drop.

It's Time for Dinner

Before the kids were in high school they had a set bedtime - now, they turn in after one of their favorite shows. Saying grace before dinner is expected. There is no television before homework is done. Yard work is what they do as contributing members of the family and doesn't pay - either does emptying the dishwasher, putting out the trash or walking the dog. There's no going out on school nights. When challenged by "competing forces" we respond, "Because that's just the way it is!" Do you have "rules" or built-in structures to keep your family priorities in line?

Remember! You may not be the one who schedules gymnastics classes or soccer practice over the dinner hour or church service, but you do get to decide whether or not to register your children for those class times! You get to make choices and be the manager of your life.

Organizational Skills

The last component of self-discipline is the ability to organize your life so as to manage your time. When you are in a complete state of chaos, you send the message time controls you. Your disorganization translates as poor self-management skills and serves as an Individual Detractor. Inherent in self-discipline is doing what you need to do to when it ought to be done! I find getting the tasks I don't want to do done first, such as making phone calls, is a form of self-discipline that allows me to get on with my day. Below is a brief look at some of my favorite organizational strategies.

Tips for Enhanced Organizational Strategies:

- Only handle a piece of mail once before acting on it.
- Open your mail over a garbage can to immediately discard unwanted materials.
- Set aside the same time every day to make phone calls and return calls.
- Get your house working for you at the beginning of every day.
- Never go to bed with dishes in your sink (i.e. no unfinished business).
- Use bulletin boards for frequently referenced information.
- Keep the same kind of filing system at home as you would at work.
- File – don't pile!
- Use your daily planner to forecast time commitments.
- Create effective systems of organization (i.e. neat, well-labeled storage boxes).
- Delegate tasks to those more qualified or whose responsibility dictates (i.e. kids clean up their own messes).

INFLUENCE 20 INITIATIVES

- Rent Forrest Gump and watch it.
- Make a list of self-discipline behaviors.
- Read the autobiographies of great leaders – their stories contain enormous sacrifice, discipline, and commitment.
- Set a small goal with a short deadline. Once you do what you said you would do, increase the goal and increase the deadline.
- Enlist someone to check the progress of a goal you've set.
- Identify a self-imposed reward for not doing something today you'd normally do.
- Identify a self-imposed reward for doing something today you normally wouldn't do.
- Make a list of your behaviors showing a lack of self-discipline.
- Keep a record of successful acts of self-discipline.
- Clearly delineate between a lack of self-discipline and an addiction.
- If you have an addiction, seek professional help.
- Make the connection between self-discipline and self-esteem. Do you feel worthy of improvement and making a difference in this world?
- Choose one thing that you are going to turn into a routine or habit and do it every day.

Chapter 29

INSIGHT TWENTY-ONE
The Hand of Humility

"I never did anything alone.
Whatever was accomplished in this country
was accomplished collectively."
- Golda Meir

Remember the Boston Celtics of the Eighties? Larry Bird, Kevin McHale, Bill Walton... now that was a team! They were good. They knew they were good. They played like they knew they were good. Being a Celtic fan (and even if you weren't) you had to admire their skill – they had the talent to back up their confidence. They not only played basketball, they entertained. They played against their opponents both physically and psychologically. The courtside antics, silliness, and intensity made the Boston Garden a magical place. You got caught up in what it felt like to be a winner.

Back then, things like the three-point shooting and slam dunk contests were new. You saw moves you didn't think were possible. One of my favorite memories was watching Larry

Bird warm up for the three-point contest without taking off his warm-ups. He didn't miss a shot. When it was time for the actual contest, he still didn't take off his warm-ups. Why should he? He was Larry Bird and he was going to win. He won.

Larry Bird was that good. Despite the fact that a thin line exists between "cockiness" and "confidence," Larry Bird's actions and words happen to be true. According to Charles Spurgeon's definition of humility, speaking the truth is at the core of humility: "Humility is to make a right estimate of oneself." However, not too many people can pull off cockiness with style – unless, of course, you played for the Champion Boston Celtics! My rule of thumb is to risk being humble. There's only one Larry Bird.

The Era of Humility

Humility is the "new age" charisma. There is incredible power in giving praise where praise is due, allowing others to shine, and experiencing the personal satisfaction of making the world a better place because you've been here. Reported in the Harvard Business Review article *"Are You Picking the Right Leaders,"* researchers James Brant and Melving Sorcher claim, "We have found that many exceptional leaders are modest and display little ambition, even though on the inside they are fiercely competitive. In fact, a high degree of personal humility is far more evident among exceptional leaders than is raw ambition."

When you make humility part of your life and leadership, you literally transform "charisma" from the self-serving "Hey, look at me!" paradigm to this thing called, Zing!. Instead of focusing on what's best for you, there's a shift to focusing on what's best for the greater good. One of the most humble people I have the honor of knowing is Dr. Maureen Hartford, president of Meredith College in Raleigh, North Carolina.

Zing! Profile on Humility

I met Dr. Hartford over twenty years ago while working at Case Western Reserve University in Ohio. I was right out of graduate school and she was the dean of students. Despite her position of authority over me, I always felt comfortable in her presence. Her style of leadership was to develop the leaders around her. She was available, encouraging, inspiring, and genuinely interested in my life. Since then, I have observed and admired Dr. Hartford's professional advancement, leadership, and work on behalf of advancing opportunities for women. When asked about her accomplishments, Dr. Hartford responded by quoting Golda Meir (see opening quote). Then she humbly said, "I will tell you about some collective accomplishments." She proudly spoke of hosting one of the first AmeriCorps programs in the country while at the University of Michigan and developing campus-based LeaderShape programs at forty campuses through out the country.

I asked Dr. Hartford to define success. She said, "Success is doing what you enjoy doing and enjoying what you do." I also asked her to define happiness. She responded, "Happiness can come from many sources for me; being with family and friends, meeting new people, having an interesting discussion, reading a book, walking in the sunshine, hugging my cat, meeting a goal I have set, laughing at a good joke, and breaking 90 in golf." She summarized happiness, however, as "balance in my life." Finally, I inquired about her source of strength. She humbly responded, "I find inspiration in each of the women and men I now serve."

Learning Humility

Mahatma Gandhi said, "One must become as humble as the dust before he can discover truth."

Like the other twenty insights, humility can be learned or it may come naturally to you. As a speaker, I find it the hardest Insight taught in this book. First, humility requires honesty – sometimes the painful kind. Secondly, humility isn't easy for a speaker who makes her living on stage or as the center of attention. I've learned, however, one of the best ways to learn about being more humble is to observe (and befriend) influential leaders who demonstrate humility. You can find them if you look hard enough. They are the ones who display the following attributes of humility discussed below.

Ask yourself the tough questions. I frequently have to stop and ask myself: Which direction is my arrow pointing – from me to others or from others to me? Have I been focusing on "what's in it for me?" or "what can I do for you?" By literally replacing your "I" thinking and language with "we" or "you" thinking and language, you will begin to be received as more humble. This technique downplays your own importance.

Serve others graciously. Accept your place in the world. If/when you see yourself as a teacher, you will teach. If/when you see yourself as a servant, you will serve with honor. If/when you see yourself as a mentor, you will mentor. Sharing your talents (as opposed to selfishly using them for your own advancement) is an act of humility.

Leadership in the 21st century is not about one person. In fact, I believe today's organizational leader should make themselves replaceable! They should strive to train at least three people who could replace them at any moment. This is way too threatening for the "look at me" kind of charisma, but exactly the kind of "charizmatic" leadership needed to

Zing!

change the world. Shared leadership – while maintaining an articulated vision for all leaders – is the new model of influential leadership. Your willingness to be replaced is a sign of your true worth!

Practice being modest. Someone once said, "Modesty is the art of drawing attention to whatever it is you are being humble about." You may be the "brains" of your organization, but are you smart enough to give everyone else the credit? Share the praise and look for ways to honor others for their contributions. Whenever possible, avoid self-serving awards and the need to tell others about your latest accomplishments (unless in your inner circle) if it doesn't make them feel better about themselves or serve an inspirational function. If you do find yourself on the receiving end of well wishing individuals, then be grateful and be graceful. Allow the good-doers to praise you, and find a way to maximize your appreciation for their efforts and thoughtfulness. You show grace by deflecting their good wishes towards you back onto them. When accepting praise, remember to keep your remarks brief.

Remain open for discussion. Be open to others' thoughts and welcome them. Solicit others' opinions while maintaining the final word. Here's a humbling fact: Some people are smarter than you and will have better "wicked-good ideas" than you! Remember to pay special attention to voices of dissension because they will make you think the hardest. If you surround yourself with "Yes People" you have succeeded in meeting your needs, not those of the greater good. Better yet, surround yourself with great counsel and people who are smarter than you are! Don't be threatened by them; embrace their ideas and knowledge. Learn from them. It takes a great deal of humility to be open for discussion. Others will admire your willingness to be accurate and informed.

Stop saying arrogant things. Many of my colleagues also struggle with humility. In fact, a fellow speaker recently told me that he doesn't read program evaluations. "Why should I?" he snapped, and bragged about how many speeches he gives a year, suggesting that his audience aren't professional speakers and thus don't have a valid opinion. This speaker no longer speaks. Confidence is essential to a high ZQ, but not when it crosses the line and becomes arrogance. Anytime you have the opportunity to be formally evaluated, take it! How else are you going to know what works and what needs work?

Admit your mistakes. Be willing to admit you made a mistake or were wrong. The world won't come to an end. Everybody makes mistakes because we aren't perfect. That's just the way it is. However, when you do or say something in poor judgment, forget to show up, or fail to prepare as needed, you actually show more humility by admitting your mistake instead of covering it up. Owning your mistakes is significant to Zing!; lying and/ or blaming others are Individual Detractors. Failure is not a person; it's a process. You are not a failure; you failed. It's OK to make mistakes. Once you have admitted you erred, you can do something about it. Humility invites you to be human.

People often ask me if saying "I'm sorry" is a sign of weakness. If caring about other human beings is a sign of weakness, then we are all in big trouble! It's worth repeating, saying "I'm sorry" will open more doors than saying "I'm right." Apologizing or asking for forgiveness is a sign of security and strength. It's hard for someone with a lot of ego to admit to being wrong. What's more important to you?

INFLUENCE 21 INITIATIVES

- Give equal access of your time to everyone.
- Don't ask someone to do anything you wouldn't do.
- Take calls without screening them.
- Share the credit for your success with those who made it possible.
- Avoid bragging.
- Talk less about yourself.
- Be genuinely interested in what someone else has to say.
- Give up your First Class seat to a staff member who never rides in First Class.
- Don't assume things are owed to you because of your "status."
- Stand when others walk into a room.
- Offer your name in introduction and don't presume others already know it.
- Share the perks of your position or influence.
- Pitch in when help is needed, regardless of your job or title.
- Point out the efforts of others for no apparent reason.
- To quote Ken Blanchard, "Catch someone doing something right."

Chapter 30

Serving a Greater Good

"When you make a difference in someone else's life,
your life will be forever different."
- Nancy Hunter Denney

To have read this book is to admit your life has meaning, or that you are seeking to give it greater meaning. You do want happiness and to make this world a better place because of your presence. With this realization comes the conclusion of part one of your journey; you need to believe in yourself before anyone else will believe in you! There is no escaping your call to leadership – big or small. I hope my words have inspired you to act.

Words can do that. They can make you different, especially when you act on them. I first saw the following quote by Dr. Martin Luther King, Jr. on a billboard over twenty years ago: "Anyone can be great because any one can serve." I had to pull over, write it down, and allow his words to influence my life. It was a gift I didn't need at the time, but later became the answer to many questions about my purpose in life. Whether you accept it or not, you have positive messages of inspiration coming at you all day long. They are there. Do you see them? Even the thoughts you create continue to shape you and your future.

The Future is Yours to Create

You are proof that America in the 21st century isn't void of leadership. It has been re-defined and re-shaped from a search for "heroes" to those who touch our lives daily. From teachers to students, brothers to sisters, parents to children, corporate America to community organizations – you are the future. Once you truly embrace this fact of life, you are in the next part of your journey: shifting the focus of your conversations and efforts from you to the collective we.

It's time to not only leave your fingerprints wherever you go, it's time to realize your fingerprints will most likely cover up the set left before you arrived. And yours too, will eventually be covered up by someone else's efforts to make the world a better place. It will take a collective effort to make the world a better place. One person can make a difference, but a group of dedicated individuals can work miracles. How can you inspire others to act? Your life is a gift, are you ready to give it to others? Are you ready to love your neighbor's kids like your own, commit to a cause, start a volunteer effort in your company, and encourage others to put into action what they have in their hearts?

Zing! is the means to all these possibilities and more, because despite an entire book and lots of words devoted to the topic, in its purest form Zing! is possibility. It is an endless supply of all the things that make our life and leadership possible – including (but not limited to) the twenty-one Insights from The Opportunity for Self-inspection to The Hand of Humility. There is no final chapter to your life and leadership, only the possibility of a legacy, when you strive to override competing forces to positively influence others towards a greater social good.

When you accept this fact of life, you will always know the answer to the question: What time is it?

It's Our Time

From the faith of Mother Teresa to the humor of Bob Hope - it's our time.

From the courage of Gloria Steinem to the diligence of Mia Hamm - it's our time.

From the compassion of Mr. Rogers to the vision of Bill Gates - it's our time.

From the power of Dr. Martin Luther King to the courage of Rosa Parks - it's our time.

From the humanity of Jimmy Carter to the persuasiveness of Elizabeth Dole - it's our time.

From the honor of Sandra Day O'Connor to the magnetism of Oprah Winfrey - it's our time.

From the optimism of little girls and boys who begin as scouts, to the leadership of men and women who serve as coaches, teachers and community volunteers - it's our time.

From the sacrifice of children who take care of their aging parents to the voices of those who speak up for the homeless - it's our time.

From the servitude of the men and women fighting in our armed services to the self-inspection of a nation - it's our time.

From the young to the old,

From the tall to the short,

From the front row to the back row,

From the right wing to the left wing - and every Zing! in between,

From the opportunity to make a difference in this world to the obligation,

From my words to your meaning, You - and only you, my friends - will decide how high to climb, Because now -exclamation point required - it's our time!

Exploration: The Inventory of Influence

There are two parts to this inventory. The first part examines how you perceive your use of the influence indicators. The second part examines how someone else with whom you interact on a regular basis perceives your use. The results will be more accurate – and helpful – if both parts are completed. A POST-TEST is found at the conclusion of this Appendix.

Directions: Using the three columns from the left ("Do You?"), place a check-mark under A (Always), S (Sometimes), or N (Never) to indicate the frequency or consistency with which you apply each characteristic of influence. To make this a useful assessment, enlist someone you trust and ask him/her to use the far right three columns ("Does He/She?") to rate their feelings about the frequency you employ each item.

Characteristics of Influence:	Do You?			Does He/She?		
	A	S	N	A	S	N
Exhibit sensitivity to others' needs						
Show appreciation for others' services						
Encourage others to grow						
Compliment others and wanting nothing in return						
Engage others in conversation						
Bring positive energy to projects						

Characteristics of Influence:	Do You?			Does He/She?		
	A	S	N	A	S	N
Accurately perceive environmental constraints						
Take personal risks						
Seek opportunities to expand personal skill set						
Handle adversity with grace						
Show consideration towards others						
Effectively express own desires and needs						
Actively listen to the true meaning of a message						
Praise others in public						
Demonstrate acts of kindness						
Possess a well articulated vision of the future						
Read for self-improvement						
Engage in exercise regime						
Dress appropriately for any given setting						
Incorporate fair play into all interactions						

Characteristics of Influence:	Do You?			Does He/She?		
	A	S	N	A	S	N
Count your/his/her blessings						
Remember others' names						
Refrain from finishing others' sentences						
Set high standard of personal conduct						
Cover your/his/her mouth when yawning						
Use proper table manners and table etiquette						
Possess an optimistic outlook on life						
Manage distractions in your/his/her environment						
Act with modesty						
Exercise self-control						
Use your/his/her time constructively						
Effectively prioritize daily tasks						
Effectively manage your/his/her energy						
Build upon personal strengths						

Characteristics of Influence:	Do You?			Does He/She?		
	A	S	N	A	S	N
Keep confidences						
Show gratitude for advantages in life						
Make others feel valued in your/his/her presence						
Always tell the truth						
Create opportunities to network						
Utilize others' talents towards a common goal						
Believe in a greater force other than you/him/her						
Show enthusiasm for life and leadership						
Deal effectively with adversity						
Speak well at the podium or publicly						
Find the humor in difficult situations						
Possess a sense of playfulness						
Refrain from speaking negatively of others						
Arrive on time to commitments						

Characteristics of Influence:	Do You? A	S	N	Does He/She? A	S	N
Initiate small talk with strangers						
Earn the respect of others						
Nurture others to grow and become better people						
Willingly take self-assessments						
Accept feedback on performance well						
Practice humility and modesty						
Trust others before they give you reason not to						
Possess a strong work ethic						
Encourages others' ideas and involvement						
Possess a network of quality contacts						
Think before speaking						
Make others feel comfortable						

Add column TOTALS: ___ ___ ___ ___ ___ ___

X 2 X1 X0 X2 X1 X0

___ + ___ = ___   ___ + __ = __

Scoring: Give yourself **2 points** for every A response. Give yourself **1 point** for every S response and **0 points** for N responses. Do this for both your responses and your evaluator's. You will end up with two totals. Compare each total with the analysis below, keeping in mind it's other's opinions of you that provide the most accurate information.

If either total is less than 60: You are reading the right book! Pay considerable attention to those factors that influence others' perception of you. Although you may show strength in some characteristics, you should take advantage of all of the skill-building opportunities in this book, including self-assessments. You are encouraged to discuss the observations of your evaluator.

If either total is between 61 and 100: You are still reading the right book! Pay attention to whether you scored closer to 61 or closer to 100. The range accounts for the fact others' perceptions may have more or less significance, depending upon the nature of your relationship and the extent to which they are able to observe all of the listed traits. This score suggests you actively work on improving your skill sets and have an interest in being happier. For best results, seek out the Insights and accompanying skill building lessons in each chapter. Focus on one Insight a week. Practice makes perfect!

If either total is over 100: Zing! is your thing! Your ability to influence others is quite high. Still, attend to those traits to which your evaluator responded with S or N, even if you disagree with him/her. Do you see a common factor or pattern among those responses? Is it possible you don't practice those traits on a regular basis?

APPENDIX B

Exploration: A Matter of Attitude

Directions: Indicate whether the statements below are true (T) or false (F) on the space provided. Do you...

_____ Think about how to reach your goals.
_____ Point out others' faults.
_____ Speak negatively about yourself.
_____ Think that every day is a new day.
_____ Marvel at the stupidity surrounding you.
_____ Believe in your potential.
_____ Dislike being asked, "How are you?" because the person asking really doesn't care.
_____ Question why someone is being nice to you.
_____ Offer to help others.
_____ Notice the goodness in others.
_____ Often wonder, "What's in this for me?"
_____ Know that when something breaks, it can usually be fixed.
_____ Take responsibility for your state of mind.
_____ Ask complete strangers, "How are you?" then listen to what they say.
_____ Believe others are waiting for you to fail so they can point it out to you.
_____ Would send yourself flowers if no one else was going to and you wanted flowers.
_____ Have no goals or dreams because they won't ever come true.
_____ Blame others for the way you get treated by them.
_____ Value the day.
_____ Would never want a friend to send you a small gift.
_____ Live for 5pm, weekends and vacations.
_____ Think you have high self-esteem.

_____ See little meaning in what you do.
_____ Think motivational books are pointless.
_____ Laugh at your own stupidity.
_____ Think about ways to motivate yourself from the inside out.

Scoring:
Row 1: Circle which statements above you marked false: 2,3, 5,7,8,11,15,17,18,20,21,23,24

Row 2: Circle which statements above you marked true: 1,4,6, 9,10,12,13,14,16,19,22,25,26

Record the amount of numbers circled in Row 1 = _____

Record the amount of numbers circles in Row 2 = _____

Add both rows to achieve your TOTAL SCORE: _____

Interpretation:
Total score is between 22-26: This score suggests a very upbeat and positive attitude about life in general. You enjoy people and your perception of your environment reflects a high level of self-esteem allowing you to achieve any of your goals and work effectively with others – all YOU have to do is make the effort! Your attitude is a "Can Do" attitude.

Total score is between 14-22: This score suggests there's room for improvement. You are still relying on external sources of motivation as a means of making yourself happy. Work on owning your own perceptions. Don't be afraid to treat yourself better by cleaning the lens you use to view life. Look for the small pleasures and gifts. There is plenty of room for a more productive attitude. Look inward and trust your potential.

Total score is between 0-13: This score suggests a significant amount of negativity in your outlook on life. Until you change the way you look at your environment, your glass will always be half empty. Remember, the energy you put out there is the energy you get to draw from! You do care about you – or you wouldn't be reading this book! Believe you deserve happiness.

Exploration: The Art of Communicating

Directions: Like previous assessments around influence and charisma, soliciting information about how your skills are perceived by others is more important (and accurate) than getting you opinion. Under "Do YOU?" check if you practice a particular skill always (A), sometimes (S), or never (N). Invite someone who interacts with you to do the same under "Does He/She?" as they perceive you to carry out the following traits of effective communication.

	Do You?			Does He/She?		
	A	S	N	A	S	N
Hear what isn't being said?						
Listen to the emotion behind words?						
Maintain eye-contact during conversations?						
Paraphrase (repeat comment to person in own words)?						
Make strangers comfortable with small talk?						
Confront in private?						

	Do You?			Does He/She?		
	A	S	N	A	S	N
Manage your emotions during confrontation?						
Change others' behaviors through confrontation?						
Follow up when you say you'll follow up?						
Write clearly?						
Possess a growing vocabulary?						
Sound intelligent?						
Use grammar correctly?						
Match your words to your body language?						
Refrain from speaking over someone else's words?						
Let silence happen?						
Rearrange a room so people can network better?						
Sit when talking to someone of a different height?						

	Do You?			Does He/She?		
	A	S	N	A	S	N
Refrain from raising your voice in disagreement?						
Express your thoughts accurately?						
Challenge inappropriate remarks?						
Stand when meeting someone?						
Stand up for your own rights to an opinion?						
Protect others' rights to disagree with you?						
Control for various types of "noise" in conversations?						

Interpretation:

Instead of adding the number of responses in each column, it will be more productive to discuss the discrepancy of markings with your evaluator. Use the responses to ask more questions and further consider which areas of communication need improvement.

Exploration: Public Speaking Homework

Directions: Use the following questions to evaluate a speaker or professor. Run off a few copies before writing on it. Use this form to gain valuable feedback about your abilities. Every time you observe an attribute of an effective speaker, place a check mark next to it.

Trait:	Frequency of Use				
Compliments audience					
Smiles					
Laughs at self					
Expresses appreciation to the audience					
Lets silence happen					
Asks a question and listens to the answer					
Interacts with audience prior to taking the podium					
Leaves the podium during speech					
Uses a personal story to make a point					

Trait:	Frequency of Use				
Quotes someone famous					
Tells an appropriate joke					
Changes course when audience isn't reacting					
Uses PowerPoint presentation as a back-up of major points					
Identifies five or less major points					
Uses another medium to make or support a point					
Visually demonstrates or supports a point					
Uses hand gestures					
If he/she strays from outline gets back on track					
References additional sources of information					
Faces right, left, and center audience equally					
Let's go of material not covered if running out of time					
Appears to be having fun					

Zing!

Trait:	Frequency of Use				
Handles difficult questions appropriately					
Admits to not knowing an answer					
Clarifies a question if no one responds					
Uses silence effectively					
Makes sexist, oppressive, or defensive remarks					
Makes a self-serving comment (speaks out of ego)					
Apologizes for being "bad" or not knowing something					
Points out when he/she has lost his/her place					
Uses a distracting body movement or word (i.e. "um")					
Uses sarcasm to make a point					

Grade the Speaker:

a. On a scale of 1 (awful) to 10 (exceptional) how did this presentation rate in your eyes? _____

b. On a scale of 1 (insignificant) to 10 (worthy) how did this speaker make you feel? _____

Follow Up Questions:

- *How would you describe the speaker's perceptiveness to his/her audience?*
- *What methods did the speaker use to engage his/her audience?*
- *How did the speaker respond if the audience appeared to not respond?*
- *What various methods of instruction were used to make points?*
- *What five or less points were made?*
- *How effectively was the speaker's content presented?*
- *How well did the speaker use visual aids?*
- *How did the speaker handle questions?*
- *What did the speaker do to persuade the audience to listen to his/her point of view?*
- *What did the speaker do to demonstrate his/her confidence?*

Zing!

Appendix E

Community Opportunities and Resources

The Big Brothers Big Sisters of Greater New Bedford, MA
The Big Brothers Big Sisters program, a component of Child and Family Services, is a nationally recognized mentor program that has been serving millions of children since 1904. Big Brothers Big Sisters of Greater New Bedford, MA is committed to improving the lives of children by matching them with one to one supported relationships with adult volunteers. Volunteers range in age from 17 to retirement with diverse social, economic, and cultural backgrounds. The children benefit from the program by having someone special to spend time with and enjoy. As a result, their self esteem and school performance are enhanced. Specifically, children with mentors are 52% less likely to skip a day of school, 33% less likely to become involved in violence, and 46% less likely to start using drugs.

Consider becoming a volunteer in your local community or help support the children in New Bedford, MA by sending a financial donation to Child and Family Services of New Bedford, Big Sister Big Brother Program, 800 Purchase Street, New Bedford, MA 02740. For more information contact: 508-990-0894.

Edward L Urbanowski Memorial Fund
The Eddie L. Urbanowski Memorial Fund was established by his family to assist other families in covering non-reimbursable expenses associated with caring for their children undergoing cancer treatment. Currently, the fund is being used to assist in parking fees at UMASS Memorial Hospital in Worcester, MA.

Edward L. Urbanowski (Eddie) died on October 26, 2003 after a four year battle with Leukemia. He was twelve years old. Donations can be made in his name to: Barre Savings Bank, Pleasant Street, Paxton, MA 01612. To reach the bank directly, call: 508-799-2274.

Alternatives in Motion

Founded by author, speaker and friend, Johnnie Tuitel in 1995, Alternatives in Motion is based upon the belief everyone should have the opportunity to participate in society and not be hindered by mobility issues. Alternatives in Motion provides wheelchairs to people who need them but cannot afford them, and don't qualify for any other financial assistance. You can help by volunteering, donating a wheelchair or making a financial contribution. To learn more about how you can make a difference, visit: www.alternativesinmotion or contact George Ranville at 877-468-9335.

Notes

CHAPTER 6
[1] Rakesh Khurana, "The Curse of the Superstar CEO," *Harvard Business Review*, September 2002, 60.
[2] Ibid.
[3] Jay A. Conger, Rabindra N. Kanungo, and Sanjay T. Menon, "Charismatic leadership and follower effects," *Journal of Organizational Behavior*, **21**, 2000, 747-767.

CHAPTER 9
[1] Referenced in Richard Boyatzis, Annie McKee, and Daniel Goleman, "Reawakening Your Passion for Work," *Harvard Business Review*, April 2002, 91.

CHAPTER 10
[1] Martin Luther King, Jr., *A Call to Conscience: The Landmark Speeches of Dr. Martin Luther King, Jr.* (New York: Warner Books, 2001, 145-146.

CHAPTER 17
[1] Go to http://www.redenvelope.com to send gifts for any occasion.

CHAPTER 20
[1] CASA stands for Court Appointed Special Advocate. According to their website: "In the United States over one half million children cannot safely live with their families. A CASA volunteer serves an abused or neglected child." You can learn more about CASA by visiting: www.nationalcasa. org. A brief history of CASA is also taken directly from their website:

Concerned over making decisions about abused and neglected children's lives without sufficient information, a Seattle judge conceived the idea of using trained community volunteers to speak for the best interests of these children in court. So successful was this Seattle program that soon judges across the country began utilizing citizen advocates. In 1990, the U.S. Congress encouraged the expansion of CASA with passage of the Victims of Child Abuse Act. Today more than 900 CASA programs are in operation, with 70,000 women and men serving as CASA volunteers. CASA is an acronym for Court Appointed Special Advocate.

CHAPTER 25
[1] Jay A. Conger, Rabindra N. Kanungo, and Sanjay T. Menon, "Charismatic leadership and follower effects," *Journal of Organizational Behavior*, **21**, 2000, 747-767.

CHAPTER 26
[1] Steve Allen, *How to Be Funny*, (New York: Prometheus Books, 1998), 57.

CHAPTER 27
Fred Rogers, *The World According to Mister Rogers: Important Things to Remember*, (New York: Hyperion, 2003), 183.

Warren G. Bennis and Robert J. Thomas, *Geeks & Geezers*, (Boston: Harvard Business School Press, 2002), 20. Neoteny is defined as the "retention of youthful qualities by adults."

Bibliography

Allen, Steve. *How to Be Funny: Discovering the Comic in You*. New York: Prometheus Books, 1998.

Allesandra, Tony. *Charisma*. New York: Warner Books, 1998.

Bennis, Warren G. and Robert J. Thomas. *Geeks and Geezers: How Era, Values, and Defining Moments Shape Leaders*. Boston: Harvard Business School Press, 2002.

Bolemann, Lee G. and Terrence E. Deal. *The Wizard and the Warrior*. John Wiley & Sons, Inc., 2006.

Buckingham, Marcus and Donald O. Clifton, Ph.D. *Now, Discover Your Strengths*. New York: The Free Press, 2001.

Buckingham, Marcus and Curt Coffman. *First, Break All The Rules*. New York: Simon & Schuster, 1999.

Chopra, Deepak. *The Seven Spiritual Laws of Success*. California: Amber-Allen Press, 1994.

Carnegie, Dale. *Lifetime Plan for Success*. New York: Galahad Books, 1984.

Carter, Jimmy. *Living Faith*. New York: Random House, 1998.

Clinton, William Jefferson. *Giving: How Each of us can Change the World*. New York: Random House, 2007.

Conger, Jay A., Rabindra N. Kanungo, and Sanjay T. Menon, "Charismatic leadership and follower effects," *Journal of Organizational Behavior*, **21**, 2000, 747-767.

Conger, Jay A. Rabindra N. Kanungo, Sanjay T Menon, and Purnima Mathur, "Measuring charisma: Dimensionality and validity of the Conger-Kanungo scale of charismatic leadership," *Revue Candienne des Sciences del"Administration*, Sep 1997.

Covey, Stephen R. *The 7 Habits of Highly Effective People*. New York: Simon & Schuster, 1989.

Crant, Michael J, and Thomas S. Bateman, "Charismatic leadership viewed from above: the impact of proactive personality, " *Journal of Organizational Behavior*, **21**, February 1999, 63.

Darling, Diane. *The Networking Survival Guide: Get the Success You Want by Tapping into the People You Know*. New York: McGraw-Hill, 2003.

Friedman, Thomas L. *The World is Flat*. Farrar, Straus and Giroux, 2006.

Gardner, John W. *On Leadership*. New York: The Free Press, 1990.

Gaudiani, Claire. *The Greater Good: How Philanthropy Drives the American Economy and Can Save Capitalism*. New York: Time Books, 2003.

George, Elizabeth. *Life Management for Busy Women: Living Out God's Plan with Passion and Purpose*. Oregon: Harvest House Publishers, 2002.

Glickman, Ph.D, Rosalene. *Optimal Thinking*. New York: John Wiley & Sons, Inc., 2002.

Greenleaf, Robert. *Servant Leadership: A Journey into the Nature of Legitimate Power and Greatness*. New York: Paulist Press, 1977.

Hall, Doug. *Jump Start Your Brain*. New York: Warner Books, 1995.

Harrell, Keith. *Attitude is Everything: 10 Life-Changing Steps to Turning Attitude into Action*. New York: HarperCollins Publishers, 2003.

King, Jr., Ph.D., Martin Luther. *A Call to Conscience: The Landmark Speeches of Dr. Martin Luther King, Jr.* New York: Warner Books, 2001.

Komives, Susan R., Nance Lucas and Timothy R. McMahon. *Exploring Leadership: For College Students Who Want to Make a Difference*. New York: Jossey-Bass. 2006.

Kouzes, James M. and Barry Z. Posner. *A Leader's Legacy*. New York: Jossey-Bass. 2006

Loehr, Jim and Tony Schwartz. *The Power of Full Engagement*. New York: Free Press.

Lundin, Ph.D., Stephen C., John Christensen and Harry Paul. *Fish! For Life*. New York: Hyperion Books.

Lama, His Holiness The Dali. *The Art of Happiness: A Handbook for Living*. New York: Riverhead Books. 1998.

Maxwell, John C. *Talent is Never Enough*. Nashville, TN: Thomas Nelson, In. 2007.

Maxwell, John C. The 17 Essential Qualities of a Team Player. Nashville, TN: Thomas Nelson, Inc. 2002

Maxwell, John C. *The 21 Irrefutable Laws of Leadership*. Nashville, TN: Thomas Nelson, Inc.,1998.

Maxwell, John C. *The Difference Maker.* Nashville, TN: Thomas Nelson, Inc., 2006.

Nelson, Bob. *1001 Ways to Reward Employees*. New York: Workman Publishing, 1994.

O'Neil, William J. *Business Leaders & Success*. New York: McGraw-Hill, 2004.

Peck, M.D., M. Scott. *Further Along The Road Less Traveled*. New York: Simon & Schuster, 1993.

Pink, Daniel H. *A Whole New Mind*. Penguin Books Inc. 2005.

Roane, Susan. *How to Work a Room*. New York: HarperCollins Publishing, 2002.

Robbins, Anthony. *Awaken The Giant Within*. New York: Simon & Schuster, 1991.

Rogers, Fred. *The World According to Mister Rogers*. New York: Hyperion, 2003.

Sample, Steven B. *The Contrarian's Guide to Leadership*. California: Jossey-Bass, 2002.

Smith, Dave. *To be of use: the seven seeds of meaningful work*. California: New World Library, 2005.

Tannen, Deborah. *The Argument Culture: Moving From Debate to Dialogue*. New York: Random House, 1998.

Theresa, Mother. *A Simple Path*. New York: Ballatine Books, 1995.

Tracy, Brian. *Create Your Own Future: How to Master the 12 Critical Factors of Unlimited Success.* New York: John Wiley & Sons, Inc., 2002.

Urban, Hal. *Life's Greatest Lessons: 20 Things That Matter.* New York: Simon & Schuster, 2003.

Wielkiewicz, Richard M. "Validity of the Leadership Attitudes and Beliefs Scale: Relataionships with personality, communal orientation, and social desirability," *Journal of College Student Development*, Jan/feb 2002.

About the Author

Nancy Hunter Denney is a nationally recognized author and inspirational educator with a passion for life and leadership. In 1993, after living everyone else's definition of having it all, she resigned from administrative duties at a private engineering college to raise her own children, spend more time with her husband, start her own speaking business, and pursue her true passions in life. Nancy specializes in inspiring those who make a difference, especially non-profit helping organizations and is known for her high energy presentation style, sense of humor and passionate delivery of original content. She has appeared on over 800 college and university campuses and is a frequent keynote speaker at national, regional and state conferences in higher education, women's leadership and non-profit helping organizations. On the national stage she has appeared with Dr. Phil, Soledad O'Brien, Dana Reeves, Sarah Weddington, Amanda Gore and has enjoyed inspiring corporate clients ranging from Deloitte-Touche to Century 21.

Nancy is a founding partner of Within Reach Productions, LLC and the owner of Zing! Leadership Development Systems, LLC. She has authored two books, and co-authored three books on life and leadership. Her publishing company is dedicated to helping inspiring authors see their ideas come to life.

Nancy serves on the Christian Education committee of her church, volunteers for the Big Sister Big Brother Program, serves on the national advisory board of the National Conference of Student Leadership, and serves on the national board of the Association of College Personnel Administrators Foundation.

Nancy resides in Marion, Massachusetts with her two children, husband and dog.

For product information or to inquire about the speaking services of Nancy Hunter Denney:

Nancy Hunter Denney
Box 1041
Marion, MA 02738

Call: 888.566.7536
www.nancyhunterdenney.com

Zing! Leadership Development Systems, LLC

Zing! Leadership Development Systems, LLC was created to provide assistance in the development of creative, impactful and inspiring leadership curriculum based around the Zing! approach to teaching, living and learning leadership. A variety of inspirational products are available through the on-line store.

Contact Information:
Box 1041
Marion, MA 02738
1.888.566.7536
www.zingleadership.com

Other Books and Products
By
Nancy Hunter Denney

The Now Factors of College Success, co-authors Jermaine Davis and Michael Miller, Zing! Leadership Development Systems, LLC publisher, Marion, MA. (2008)

Lessons from the Road: Inspirational Insights by Leading Speakers in Education, Zing! Leadership Development Systems, LLC publisher, Marion, MA. (2007)

Let Your Leadership Speak: How to Lead and Be Heard (2000)

Life by Design: A Do-It-Yourself Approach to Achieving Happiness (1997), Victory Publications, Paxton, MA.

Products
DVD: *The Future is Yours to Create!* – a short collection of inspirational clips on time, love, life, leadership, and freedom.

Additional Inspirational Products: Posters, coffee mugs and T-shirts

THANK YOU FOR MAKING A DIFFERENCE!